Hydro Flask®
Let's Go!

Further.
Faster.

Never
Stood Still.

montane.com

AIRZONE ACTIVE
Feel the breeze

With its AirZone LT carry system, featuring anti-barrel plates and suspended mesh for maximum breathability, our AirZone Active packs are the perfect choice for long days outdoors when staying cool is key.

FOUNDER, PRODUCER, CREATIVE DIRECTOR
John Summerton

EDITOR
Alex Roddie

DIRECTOR OF PHOTOGRAPHY
Martin Hartley

CONTRIBUTING EDITORS
Jenny Tough
Tom Hill

SUB-EDITORS
Ben Lerwill

EDITOR AT LARGE
Andrew Mazibrada

COVER PHOTOGRAPH
Alberto Ojembarrena

SIDETRACKED ONLINE:
Website: www.sidetracked.com
Twitter: @Sidetrackedmag
Instagram: @Sidetrackedmag
Facebook: /Sidetrackedmag
Email: info@sidetracked.co.uk

Volume 21 is
kindly supported by:

Foreword

Alex Roddie

'Happiness only real when shared'

—Christopher McCandless, writing near the end of his life in the Magic Bus, Alaska

When we think of adventure, the image we conjure in our minds is often one of solitude: the lone wanderer striding through wilderness, surrounded by the glories of the natural world. An immersion and a concentration; a solitary challenge, delving inward to explore personal limits and boundaries. The literature of adventure is ablaze with these themes, from the Romantic artistic movement of the late 18th century to the heroic era of exploration, and they continue to resonate with us today. But while these are major factors in why many of us venture into the wild and do the things we do there, they aren't the whole story. Perhaps, if we're honest with ourselves, the solitary archetype in adventure is an illusion anyway.

The truth is that most journeys are team efforts. Even if you travel alone, you depend on a web of other people out of sight but not always out of mind: supporters, friends and family, chance encounters with people along the way who buoy you up and keep you going, even followers on social media. A kind gesture from a stranger, or an encouraging message from someone who wants you to succeed, can make the difference between failure and endurance. When travelling with others, this can be even more pronounced. The choice of companions can make or break a trip – and friendships forged in the crucible of adventure can be some of the most intense relationships of our lives, because out there where it really matters, where every decision can have dramatic consequences, we learn the true meaning of trust. In situations of greatest adversity, partnership is often all the more important.

I think that adventure depends on trust. On being able to count on the people you're with; on knowing that someone is looking out for you, just as you're looking out for them. Many of the stories in this issue of *Sidetracked* explore what it means to trust and depend upon someone else. In 'Polar Shadows', Vincent Colliard and Caroline Côté face the long, brutal night of the Arctic winter with little beyond their reliance on one another to keep them going. Mónica Fuentes and Alberto Ojembarrena dig deep and trust in each other's capabilities when trekking through a seldom-hiked region of Iceland, and Anna von Boetticher must place her life entirely within the hands of her companion in 'Under the Ice'. Tamara Lunger and Simone Moro touch the very limits of human endurance while attempting the first winter crossing of two 8,000m Himalayan peaks – an expedition that changes Tamara's life. Then there is the friendship between Chef Hilven and Terence Ver Angsioco, forged over beach cuisine and Instagram Live broadcasts from Coron Island. Other partnerships are more abstract but no less real. In 'Monarca', Benjamin Jordan pushes through adversity and draws strength from the monarch butterflies whose migration inspired his flight across America.

Perhaps such stories hold more currency for us now, in our changed world. Since the start of the COVID-19 pandemic, many of us have been cut off from friends, loved ones, our chosen communities – and, yes, from adventure. Maybe our long spells in the lockdown cooler have given us time to reflect on the true value of partnership and solitude alike, made us realise that we can't do it all alone. That the true value of human connection is in trust, in accomplishing things greater than ourselves.

In my own mountain adventures, I have always favoured the solo long-distance trail, the unroped climb, the lonely summit – that fabled solitary immersion in nature. But perhaps I've been missing half the picture. I hope you enjoy reading these incredible stories of endurance, ambition, and trust.

@alex_roddie

PHOTO: SIMON URWIN
STORY: SAND IN THE BLOOD // PAGE 122

THE VOID'S EDGE

STORY: TAMARA LUNGER
WRITTEN BY: MARTA MANZONI
PHOTOGRAPHY BY: MATTEO PAVANA
LOCATION: PAKISTAN

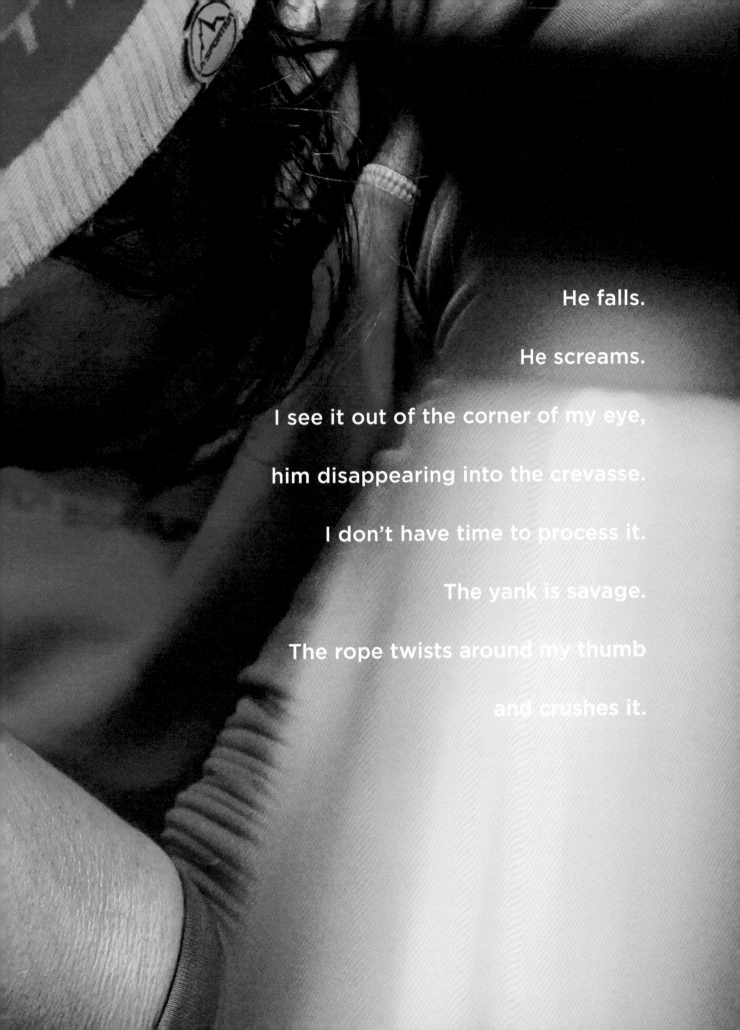

He falls.

He screams.

I see it out of the corner of my eye,

him disappearing into the crevasse.

I don't have time to process it.

The yank is savage.

The rope twists around my thumb

and crushes it.

'Come on, not Everest,' Simone says. I don't even suggest K2; I know he doesn't want to, not after his wife dreamt that he would die on an expedition to the second-highest mountain on Earth. 'Manaslu?' he counters. I say no. Simone has another idea: 'Let's link up Gasherbrum I with Gasherbrum II.'

I let this sink in. The Gasherbrum peaks. I've never been, and I always like to explore new places. It would be the first winter link-up of two 8,000ers in history. Gasherbrum I and II have already been linked during the summer, in 1984, an incredible feat by two giants of Himalayan mountaineering: Reinhold Messner and Hans Kammerlander. To me, taking on this adventure with Simone would be like a way of paying homage to Messner, our Italian King of the 8,000ers. It's decided. In December 2019, we take off from Italy, heading for Islamabad.

***

I'm excited. For the first time I'm due to leave Islamabad by plane, instead of reaching Skardu by the small bus I've used on prior expeditions. The flight gets cancelled. We re-book the plane for the next day. Flight cancelled. As it happens, I like the journey by van a lot: it's a unique experience that makes me feel alive. They tell me that in some villages along the KKH (Karakoram Highway) it's frowned upon to look out the window, but I can't resist, and I peek, filling my eyes with memories. The scent of travel: a door to dreams.

The highway is alive. Workers are trying to widen the road with jackhammers. I get off to offer them some earplugs. They refuse, but offer to trade places with me in making the holes. We wait two hours for them to blow up a bit of earth. We pass the place where Bin Laden was killed. Chicken-sellers go up and down tirelessly, showing their goods to travellers and bathing the birds so they won't die of heat and thirst. The trucks are works of art: the doors, made of wood, are carved and decorated with high reliefs in a thousand colours, and each is different from the next. Unique pieces. We buy naan and chapati from some street vendors. I devour them. Truly a delicacy!

We cross villages; someone I know greets me, calling me by name. There's a man on a pedestal, with a knife between his feet, the blade facing upwards: he takes the meat and cuts it from above. I believe I won't eat meat today. I need to pee but I'm familiar with toilets here; nature is much better. A phrase from T.S. Eliot comes to mind: 'Only those who risk going too far can possibly find out how far one can go'. We continue to skirt the river, plunging into increasingly narrow and steep canyons. After two days on the minibus, and now almost in Skardu, the environment opens up, and I finally take my first look at the mountains.

In Skardu, we redo the bags and pack everything we need. Each bag weighs 20kg: the maximum weight that a porter carries during the winter season. Accompanied by a military officer, we take a jeep and for seven hours we bounce up and down on the battered dirt roads, passing many landslides. We encounter several military checkpoints where guards repeatedly check our passports. From Askole begins the trek to approach Base Camp: about 100km. We walk for seven days, and every morning we dismantle the whole camp – the kitchen tent, the pots, everything – before putting everything back in the backpacks and walking on.

This trek is a part of the journey that I love. Porters I know from previous expeditions always greet me warmly. It doesn't matter if the porter doesn't know English; bright eyes and a shared laugh are enough to convey affection. We arrive at Base Camp after more than 10 days of adventure, just in time for New Year, and I take the home-made cookies that my grandmother gave me for Christmas out of my backpack: we're ready to celebrate!

***

I listen to the mountain and it doesn't say anything to me. There is no feeling between us. *Oh my god! What does that mean?* I'm worried, but I don't want to rush to any conclusions. I want to give myself some time. But, even in the days that follow, the connection just doesn't spark.

***   ▷▷

I listen to the mountain.
It doesn't say anything to me.

There is no feeling between us.

Oh my god!
What does that mean?

On January 1st Simone and I begin our patrol of the glacier, looking for a way to Camp 1. To make the most of the few hours of light, we start walking with the sun, so it's warmer. Every day we go up and down, up and down the glacier. Many areas are impassable, so we ask the military for a metal ladder to help us cross the voids, and we carry it with us so that we can overcome the same critical passages on our way back in the afternoon. I think we must look like chimney sweeps.

We use the track made by the military to go to their high camp, so at least on this stretch we don't sink into the snow. But the track leads us into an icy labyrinth of seracs. Every moment we have to be careful where we put our feet and pay close attention to the route. There are many technical sections with steep ice. Often, our route peters out and forces us to stop and turn around, and as we try another path through the serac maze I realise that this already feels like a struggle – and we have only advanced 150m. I stop and listen to the mountain, to the signals it sends me. Camp 1 feels unreachable.

At a certain point we meet a flat section, but I'm not fooled by appearances. I know how it works on these glaciers: at first glance it looks like an intact surface, when in reality it hides chasms every few metres. I feel like I'm walking on eggshells. I'm tense, but I have to be focused – we can't go wrong here. Carefully, we probe each step with sticks. Snow covers the crevasses, making them invisible. We change routes so many times. There is no obvious way forward.

Suddenly I feel an emptiness beneath me and everything collapses under my feet. I'm about to fall! Instinctively I throw myself to the opposite side, saving my life, and we pick ourselves up and keep plodding forward. Soon we arrive at a point where the glacier's surface is striated by countless deep crevasses, like large canyons, and Simone and I exchange a glance – how will we continue? 'The landscape has totally changed since 2011,' he tells me. That was when he made the first winter ascent of Gasherbrum II with Denis Urubko and Cory Richards. Back then, Simone took four days

to get to Camp 1. We still haven't seen it in 18 days: a direct testimony of climate change.

Our footprints, always solid and clearly visible, are our salvation; like the pebbles in the tale of Tom Thumb, they allow us to find our way home every day. Slowly we get higher and higher. On January 18th we reach 5,500m. In 18 days we have only covered 500m in altitude, but, finally, we're close to the plateau. I am breaking trail. We wear snowshoes, spreading our weight over a larger surface area of snow; this means that we sink less, and are less likely to fall into crevasses. Ahead, I see a critical step.

'Belay me, Simone,' I ask him, and I feel him pay out the rope. I pass three crevasses. I'm on a serac above Simone. The 20m of rope between us is almost out, so I tell him to wait and start manoeuvres to belay him. I'm making the buttonhole for the half-boatman knot when Simone takes the first step – and the patch of snow he's standing on collapses under his feet.

He falls. He screams. I see it out of the corner of my eye, him sliding into the crevasse, but I don't have time to process it. The yank is savage. The rope twists around my thumb and crushes it, but I have to act – and rapidly. He pulls my hand and I fly forward, like Superwoman, pulled towards the edge of the precipice. I can't stop. I have an ice axe but it seems impossible to plant; it's all happening too fast. I pray. *Please stop, stop!* I try to slow down a bit with the snowshoes, but it's no use. Finally, I stop myself by jamming my left hand into the snow, right on the edge of the chasm.

I need to set an anchor. I stick my ice axe into the snow. I have to manoeuvre using only my right hand and mouth. My thumb is supporting the weight of Simone's 70kg, plus the 20kg of his backpack. I scream. My hand hurts so fucking bad. They will certainly amputate it. 'Cut the rope if you're safe!' I yell to him, but the crevasse is not straight and he's about 20m down. We can barely hear each other. I want to get close to him but I'm afraid of falling too. *If you fall then it really is all over,* I think; I have to hold on. But I'm going to lose my hand. ▸▸

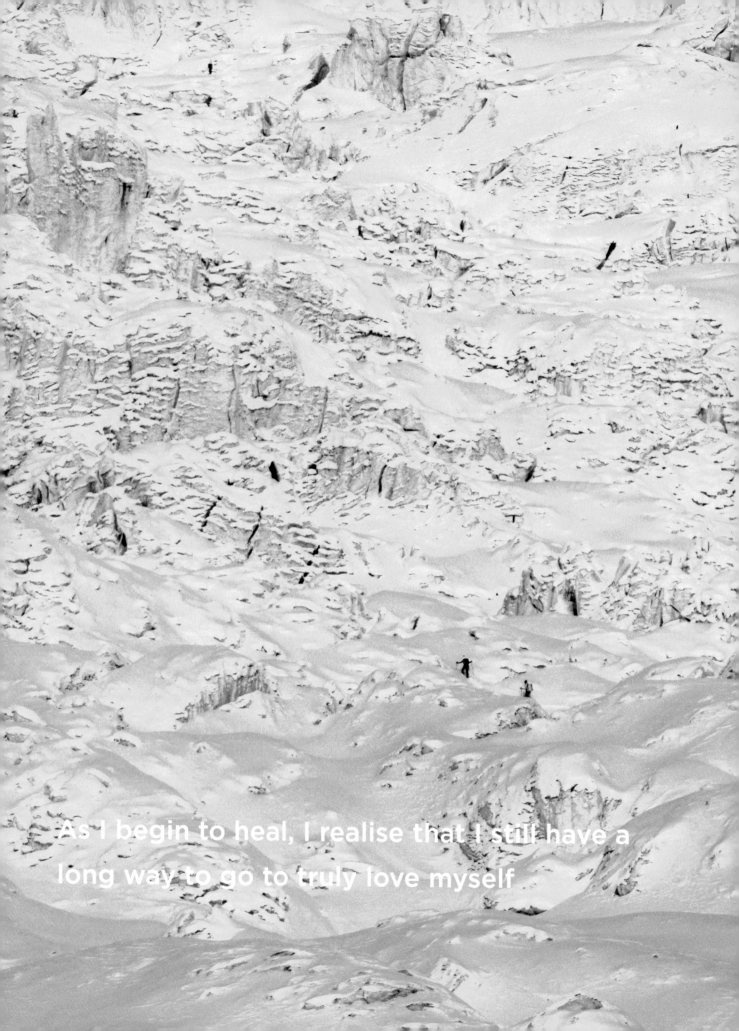

As I begin to heal, I realise that I still have a long way to go to truly love myself

'I put in an ice screw!' Simone shouts to me. I'm still very tense. My thoughts are a blurred fog through the shock and adrenaline and pain. I focus on the basics. *I'll lose my hand! I'll lose my hand! I'll lose my hand!* is the mantra that I keep screaming with my whole being. Simone takes a sling, loops it onto the ice screw, and slips his foot into it like a stirrup. The tension lessens when he unloads his weight from the rope – and at last I can free my hand. I look at my thumb. It's red, torn, and swollen. I no longer feel anything. This hand is useless, but now I have to belay Simone. I put a screw in and set a better anchor. *He is going to have to climb out by himself,* I think – there is no point in trying to make a hoist with one hand crushed.

As second climber, Simone only has one ice axe, but he will need two to climb back out. Using a trekking pole to extend my reach, I slide one of my own axes carefully down the snow slope towards him and gesture that he should use his pole to catch it. The axe skitters over the ice and picks up speed, but he manages to hook it with his pole's wrist loop and pull it towards himself. After securing the axe he takes off his snowshoes, grunting with the strain in his awkward position wedged against the ice, and puts on crampons. Fortunately, he doesn't seem to have broken anything. With great effort, after two hours, he manages to get out, climbing up with both axes and crampons, while I help him by pulling with the rope, trying to resist the waves of pain from my hand. When he reaches me, I ask him for a hug.

It's late. We have to fly back to Base Camp before dark. I carry the ladder over my head, and keep Simone on a leash, like a dog. We deserve a photo, I think, but the light has almost failed when we arrive. The cook prepares a mixture of oil and turmeric for my hand before wrapping it. I no longer feel my fingers. I don't want to go home, but I realise that there is no point in continuing with the expedition – the risk of frostbite is too high. The following day they come and pick us up by helicopter.

***

Two months after my return home I regain sensitivity to my hand. The nerves had been crushed. I'm in a black hole. I don't understand what all this means; in two out of three winter expeditions on the 8,000ers I almost didn't make it back. Does that mean I have to stop?

I go to my guru. A friend is there, and she tells me, 'Tamara, you're done. You tend to approach these things as if you were a man. If you can't listen, follow, and respect your feminine energy, you have little left to live for.' I know that she is right; this is something I have worked on a lot over the last few years, and I have already improved. But I felt more like a man when I was on the mountain, fulfilling what I think of as male roles. Breaking trail, making decisions, bullishly pushing on. Saving Simone's life, even. Simone, on the other hand, was more aware of himself – and more willing to turn back in order to avoid unnecessary risk. How can I embrace my femininity without feeling inferior? We women can achieve the same goals as men, but we have different qualities, and I must learn to respect them. As I begin to heal, I realise that I still have a long way to go to truly love myself.

@tamaralunger // @_marta_manzoni // @theverticaleye

23

Monar

c a

On the wing of a monarch butterfly

STORY: BENJAMIN JORDAN
WRITTEN BY: LYNDSAY NICOLE
PHOTOGRAPHY: BENJAMIN JORDAN & LYNDSAY NICOLE
LOCATION: UNITED STATES

To the south is a 20ft iron fence; to the north, a dry, imposing mountain. In the middle, a man with a large rucksack. Though heavy, its weight is not what holds him down.

Two months ago I was dangling from a paraglider above the clear, crisp highlands of Central Mexico. Clouds rolled in from the coast, and, without the sun's heat, I failed to find lifting air and was forced to land the kite in an alpine meadow 40km away from where I'd taken off. While packing up, I was engulfed in a swarm of insects, but not the kind I wanted to repel. Instead of swatting or spraying, I lay back in the tall grass and opened my mouth in awe. Above me were millions of monarch butterflies commuting across the meadow between a stream and dense forest. The sky, blue with orange polka dots, danced with their bright, paper-thin wings spiralling through the negative space above. Had I landed on some alien planet? I was lost in this endless moment of wonder.

These monarchs, I learned, were only days away from beginning the longest migration of any butterfly, over 3,000km, all the way to Canada. Their epic journey north takes them three full generations, but the craziest part is that a fourth generation flies all the way back – not just to Mexico, but to this very forest. Exactly how, across four generations, the tiny orange pilots manage to navigate so far from – and then back to – an area the size of a playground remains a scientific mystery to this day.

Perplexed, I dug deeper, throwing myself into scientific papers as if they were fairy tales or legends from a land before time. I was hungry for more, feeding a curiosity I hadn't felt in decades. The more I learned about the monarch the more I connected with my long-lost inner child. Mystified by the magic of this fairy-like life form, I began to question my place in the natural world, and became convinced that, if I could somehow tap into the wisdom of the monarch, I could unleash my own true potential as well.

I am the guy standing by the iron fence stretching thousands of kilometres across the desert between Mexico and the United States. I reach out to touch it, then turn to the north, never to look at it again. The dry mountain before me stands 500m tall. With my paraglider, camping gear, and two weeks' supply of peanut butter, I begin my approach.

***

My plan is straightforward: clear a launching site on top of the mountain, fly north as far as I can, and repeat for 3,000km until I reach Canada. My hope is that by simulating the monarch migration, and their natural form of free flight, I will tap into some wavelength that will open my eyes to their ancient wisdom. Not so straightforward is the overwhelming fact that a paragliding expedition of this magnitude has never been attempted. At three times further than my longest Canadian route and more than four times that of any attempt within the United States, what makes this so challenging is that paragliders require consistent weather to fly cross-country – and North America's weather is anything but.

The forecast for the next few weeks shows high wind coming from the wrong directions. Looking out over the patchwork of razor-sharp cactus-and-sagebrush landing options, I hesitate to take off into the gale and choose instead to continue clearing my launch. This morning I am relieved by the relatively light wind and, after a restless week of being grounded, am starkly aware that, if I don't make distance today, I'll be sitting out at least three more days before being granted another chance.

I check my straps, face my wing, close my eyes, and count to three. With a subtle tug of its lines, my kite pops up with refreshing enthusiasm, and a strong thermic cycle lifts my body before I even have a chance to turn around. War drums in my head beat with conviction. There will be no metres lost, no thermal spared. I'm one with nature and the only difference between me and the monarch is the combination of peanut butter and Nutella that has somehow become one with my facial hair. ▶▶

I spin desperately around a tiny column of rising air, each centimetre gained lessening the anxiety brought on by the expansive cactus fields below. An hour has passed. I am only 200m over launch, too low to go anywhere yet just high enough to realise that every creek bed within 10km is bone dry. I close my eyes, trying to feel the air. The smell of peanuts is overwhelming, and then BOOM! My climb accelerates to a heart-pounding 10m/s almost instantly. Quickly reaching 3,000m, I plan my first move as the climb continues to a whopping 5,200m, higher than I've ever been in my life. Cacti or crocodiles, drought or drenched, this is an entirely new kind of flying and any move is now a good move. *I'm a freaking astronaut!*

I skip along northbound as my luck continues. High above the desert floor, I can see mines, aqueducts, and distant mountain ranges. The sprawling city of Tucson is no larger than my boot. With days like this, I'll get to Canada in a week!

I search for answers, staring out at the 200-year-old saguaro cacti, the dry river-beds, and tumbleweeds blowing between them. They stare back with indifference, suggesting that the only thing that could ever change out here is me.

Mildly hypoxic, I land somewhere outside the ruins of Winkelman – a small mining town that was washed away by a 1993 flash flood, and the lowest point on my route at 600m. The desert heat sinks into the ghost town as if it were the drain for all things bad. All that remains alongside the river are cement foundations, a refinery with workers striking out front, and a gas station longing for better days. With mining trucks and tailings piles dotting the landscape, the rare yet polluted body of water offers a *get the hell out of here* energy – an energy also embodied by local flying conditions.

My improvised launch, a 300m ridge above the old copper refinery, is a painstakingly cleared dirt patch amidst hot rocks and a cactus salad. I've been here one week now, each evening hiking back up the mountain with 10 extra litres of water in order to avoid dehydration. My featherweight tent shelters me in my small, ridge-top clearing each night, but because of the relentless heat I have been using my sleeping bag as a pillow instead. Mornings are spent rationing water and playing my travel banjo under a shade structure I've made from cacti. I spend my afternoons getting aloft – and then invariably landing in the cacti immediately below. Without desert flying experience, I cannot grasp why, with all the heat down here, I am unable to find the thermic lift I need. Too proud to ask the local Facebook group for guidance, I remain stuck in a maddening loop.

Delirious, I glance at my watch and realise that it's already May 15th. While I've now used up 25 per cent of the flyable season, I've covered just 10 per cent of my route. This won't work. Unless something changes, I'm not going to complete this journey – and my hopes of unearthing some nugget of ancient wisdom are evaporating in the searing desert heat. I search for answers, staring out at the 200-year-old saguaro cacti, the dry riverbeds, and tumbleweeds blowing between them. They stare back with indifference, suggesting that the only thing that could ever change out here is me.

***

This first step is the hardest. Not because the 60km of flat pavement north will bring painful blisters, nor because of the heckles from pickup trucks. It's hard because, as a pioneer of fly-camp expeditions, I feel that it is up to me to set a high standard that future pilots and record-chasers will be challenged to uphold. And anyone can walk, regardless of piloting experience. Every step north feels as though I'm selling both myself and the entire paragliding community short. ▷▷

After three long days, I arrive east of Phoenix. Despite their name, and their imposing spires, the higher Superstition Mountains are more like the Canadian Rockies than anything I've seen thus far – and instil a familiar confidence. Glider, check, harness, check, cameras hanging from everywhere: check, check, and I'm airborne.

Petty grievances and fragile ego give way to giant red rocks and dagger-like grey spires. The heavy weight of my backpack now helps my glider to accelerate. The heavy weight on my heart is now a rush of endorphins surging from my brain to each of my extremities. Weightless, even if only for a few hours, I am reminded of my great purpose: to experience the freedom of the monarch butterfly. The grey spires shapeshift, moving through the parallax below. Desert lakes and cityscape become my focus as the rough air carries me to elevations that play games with my depth perception. Peering down just long enough

to witness a stealthy jumbo jet coming in to land, my grandiose emotions are rocked into perspective and I realise that, vulnerable as a butterfly, I really shouldn't be flying amongst these beasts. I make one last turn and then push full speed into the northern unknown.

***

The sun rises. From the 3,400m summit of Monroe Peak, Utah, I exit my tent and stretch my arms out with confidence and pride for the bold flights to come. After two months of negotiating short ranges, flats, and odd bumps, I am standing at the southern end of a series of expansive mountain ranges, and the birthplace of some of the longest flights in the USA.

Unlike my improvised launches in Arizona, there are actually other pilots on this one. A healthy sense of competition fills the air. With the first thermic cycles, some locals launch, making it clear that today will be windy but

from the south: perfect. I wait half an hour for the thermal tops to rise before launching, then ascend quickly to 4,000m and begin what will be my first of many tailwind transitions into the north. To my surprise, another pilot has dared to join me on this one-way journey. Both of us flying wings of similar performance, we leapfrog forward amongst the rough thermals, drifting heavily in the strong southern breeze. Sometimes I find the climb; other times it's his turn.

The features are much lower 40km north but still plenty high enough, and I lead the charge with a new-found sense of confidence. Another 5km pass and I glance back to see my wingman gaining in a steady climb about 2km behind me. I turn back quickly only to realise that the southerly gusts, now 30km/h, have other plans. I revert back north and fly like a banshee but the low windswept ridges suck me in like a butterfly in a wind tunnel. My ground speed clocking negative

▶ ▶

I revert back north and fly like a banshee but the low windswept ridges suck me in like a butterfly in a wind tunnel.

'I'm one with nature and the only
difference between me and the monarch
is the combination of peanut butter and
Nutella that has somehow become one
with my facial hair.'

10km/h, I touch down while flying backwards in a canyon east of the town of Salinas, covering about 50km in all. Exhausted, I peer up to see the other pilot, still high. That evening I'd learn that he'd flown almost four times further.

I toss and turn all night, playing out the scenarios in my head. Do I walk north, committing to the idea that my best isn't as good as I thought it was, or do I walk back south, and fly from the same peak once again, hoping to elevate my place amongst my paragliding peers? Walking north feels like resigning myself to the fact that I can't do any better, but walking south proves how badly I need to appear better than I am. Neither feels right. Now, just one third of the way into my journey, and still way behind schedule, I rest upon another fence – which, though not of iron this time, stretches across the boundaries of my undecided soul, forcing me to clearly define what kind of person I am.

Unable to measure the mighty weight of either scenario, I finish my morning coffee and, with some hesitation, begin walking north. After the first 20km, new blisters are a small token of the pain wreaking havoc within. Two days of asphalt pass below me. While bushwhacking up the west face of Salt Creek Peak, I turn around to witness all of the elevation I've gained so far and feel a tingle of excitement for what tomorrow may have in store. The sorrow of yesterday seems inexplicable now and I begin to feel a new lightness growing within me, as if I am shedding a layer of skin I didn't even realise I had been carrying around.

Although I'm only an hour in, this next flight north, towards Salt Lake City, will become one of the most satisfying and rewarding of my life. Certain at last that I've made the right choice in walking north, shame and humiliation are the next layers to be torn away in the thin air. I bounce between mountain and cloud and can feel that my difficult choice to walk north has, like an avalanche, triggered my own, true, human metamorphosis.

Four more weeks go by in the blink of an eye. Though I've only averaged about 50km per flight, I've flown almost every single day this month – and, although forced to walk here and there, it doesn't feel like such a big deal any more. I'm now three quarters of the way to Canada and have made up for all the time I lost down in Arizona.

Without hesitation, each day I am now able to hike, fly, eat, sleep, and repeat. Today I feel closer than ever to the monarch I'd hoped to understand. Once born, the monarch caterpillar must shed its skin four times before it's finally granted wings and becomes a butterfly. When identifying the greatest challenges I've faced on this journey north, from being unwilling to ask for help down in the desert to feeling like I should walk backwards in the hope of boosting my public image, the greatest threats to my success have been conceived by my ego. A transparent weight I've shouldered for most of my teenage and adult life, this heavy yet fragile cocoon is truly what distances me from the magnificence of the monarch and all other forms of life. Like a veil I've sluggishly navigated through, today I have shed this fourth layer and the path before me is crystal clear.

After 150 days in the American wilderness, Benjamin arrived at the Canadian border, completing the longest ever journey by paraglider at 2,835km. Find the documentary film, maps and photos at flymonarca.com
@benjaminjordanadventure // @pilotlyndsaynicole

THE EDGE

REINHOLD MESSNER

WORDS: HUGH FRANCIS ANDERSON // PHOTOGRAPHY: MESSNER ARCHIVES

8,000 is an insignificant number for most. Yet utter it in the presence of mountaineers and watch as their eyes light up, for the 14 peaks that exceed this number can define a lifetime. Each summit reaches like a gnarled fin towards the stratosphere and beckons the adventurous forth; with each purposeful step they ascend into the death zone, where there is not enough oxygen to sustain life for long. To climb just one of these peaks is a feat of human endurance. To summit all of them crosses another boundary altogether. So, as I wait patiently on the phone for the first person to ascend all 14 peaks to answer, my mind is awash with both awe and intrigue. I hear a heavy South-Tyrolian accent down the line, and I snap back to reality. 'Hello, this is Reinhold Messner.'

Messner was raised in South Tyrol, a culturally and politically disputed pocket of primarily German-speaking Italians in the heart of the Alps. 'I grew up in a big family of nine children in a small valley where the priest dictated what we had to do,' he tells me. 'Mountaineering was the possibility to be free. Mountaineering was my childhood.' His father, Josef, a keen hobbyist climber, first took Messner into the Alps as an infant. By the age of five, he had summited his first 3,000m peak. This natural aptitude was pushed further when his brother Günther, 20 months his junior, began climbing too. By their early teens, they were a formidable duo and soon surpassed their father. 'We did the big wall on the Kaiserspitze (3,095m), which he could not do all his years,' he chuckles even now, some 60 years later. 'We really thought we were climbers. We were so naive, but we had the instinct.'

▶ ▶

Adventure means to survive.
It is the art of surviving.

This instinct led to 500 climbing tours in the Eastern Alps, including a host of free-solo ice climbs and more than 50 first ascents, some of which have never been repeated. 'I did the most difficult rock climbing of the time. I did the most difficult ascents and the most difficult ice climbs,' he says without arrogance. 'My seventh sense, my instinct, grew by going naively into the mountains to climb big walls.' In doing so, the brothers almost single-handedly defined a renaissance of the golden age of alpinism. By the age of 18, Messner was hungry to push his boundaries further. He met Peter Habeler, with whom he would later climb Everest, and became an apprentice in advanced alpinism. 'Peter was the best at the time and taught me what I didn't know,' he says. 'In '69, I went to South America, to the Cordillera Huayhuash, and from this period on I became a high-altitude specialist.'

Messner's fateful first ascent of Nanga Parbat's Rupal Face with Günther in the spring of 1970 has been well documented. Over the years, arguments surrounding egotism, deceit, and abandonment spread through both the climbing community and mainstream media. Yet two facts remain: it marked Messner's first successful summit of an 8,000er, and it marked the death of his brother. 'That moment changed my whole life and my whole approach to the mountains,' he tells me. 'The tension, the absolute tension, was whether we could survive or not. We tried to survive, and, in the end, I was lucky, and my brother was unlucky.'

His recollection of the time is prosaic and considered. And while this event could easily have changed both his attitude and ability – he lost seven toes to frostbite – it did not, and he continued to pursue adventure. 'I knew I'd never be a good rock climber again, because without toes it's much more difficult,' he says with a chuckle, 'so I specialised in high-altitude climbing instead.' In the years that followed, he ticked off a seemingly endless series of mountaineering firsts: Everest without supplementary oxygen, Everest solo, Nanga Parbat solo; Gasherbrum I, K2, Cho You, and Dhaulagiri all in alpine style – the list goes on.

So, what drove this obsession? 'Curiosity is part of it,' he says. 'You're not addicted to it – you don't get sick if you cannot do it, but you also know you can get better spiritual and psychological experiences by doing it.' Perhaps this goes some way to explain just why he continued to push the boundaries of human endeavour; was it a spiritual and psychological battle with his antagonist, death, and the mountains as their amphitheatre? But I also wonder whether mountaineering offered a way in which to connect with his lost brother, as if each ascent became a spiritual journey to bring life into the shadowlands and closer to Günther. As he writes in *The Naked Mountain*, a first-hand account of his ascent of Nanga Parbat, 'for it was there that I experienced, quite clearly, how Life and Death first occurred... [it] remains in my memory as the story of my own death and at one and the same time the impossible story of my survival.'

Mountains have always held spiritual significance, and, for Messner, they are intertwined with what it means to be human. 'You become part of nature,' he says, 'and nature is the dictating power. When we go [to the mountains], we know without intellectual discussions; our instinct dictates what we have to do, like human beings 10,000 years ago.' Mountains offer the opportunity to reconnect with our primal being, with the raw, unrefined time when merely existing was an adventure, and this is cardinal to Messner's philosophy today. 'Adventure means to survive,' he tells me. 'It is the art of surviving.'

▶▶

Of all pursuits, mountaineering is the pinnacle of this art form, for it teeters on the edge of possibility. He explains that over the past 250 years, half of the leading climbers in the world have died in the mountains, and he's quick to add that it is not only the best who survive. He recounts the names of the late Hansjörg Auer, David Lama, Jess Roskelley, and Ueli Steck. 'For these many, many losses, there is no positive to defend our activity,' he says. 'I would never tell young people to follow me... [but] the biggest value of the mountains is to be there on your own, in your own responsibility, like adventurers thousands of years ago.'

If survival is the art form, then surely Messner is the maestro. In fear of repeating himself on the canvas of mountaineering, he turned his attention to a series of world-first overland adventures: the first longitudinal crossing of Greenland, the first crossing of Antarctica by foot, and the crossing of the Gobi and Taklamakan deserts. It's ironic, then, that a broken heel bone sustained when attempting to climb over a wall in one of his two castles signalled the end of this creative expression.

Our conversation flows into debate, and I come to learn first-hand of Messner's famously conspicuous attitude towards climbing, mountains, and those who go to them. In 1971, at the age of 26, he first expounded his opinions in *The Murder of the Impossible*, a forthright essay on the progression of climbing. 'Who has polluted the pure spring of mountaineering?' he wrote. Today, he remains as moved. 'Most climbers book their ascent of Mont Blanc or Everest,' he says. 'It is now tourism because a tourist goes to a place where there's an infrastructure and where he can enjoy his holidays.' I laugh, but I also appreciate just what impact his unfaltering thoughts have had – and what he continues to do for the mountains. He spent five years as MEP representing South Tyrol and the Italian Green Party, where he championed environmental policies. He's written countless books, produced numerous documentary and feature films, and his six Messner Mountain Museums aim to educate people on the history, culture, and ever-morphing nature of mountains. 'Nature is the rule giving dimension to life,' he says. 'Wilderness is getting less and less, and I feel a responsibility.' At 76 years old, his next expedition has nothing to do with pushing boundaries, but instead aims to bring a lifetime of knowledge to communities around the world in the hope of eliciting intrigue and change through storytelling. In evidence of this, and before our call ends, he regales me with his greatest memory from the mountains: the summit hour on K2 with Michael Dascher in 1979.

After a gruelling ascent through treacherously deep snow, Messner and Dascher reached the summit much later in the day than they had hoped. 'As we approached the last 200m, we both thought that there would be no time to reach the summit,' he says, 'but we just made it.' As they did, the last of the clouds dispersed and they sat on the peak to gaze over the limitless horizon east across China and west across Pakistan. Dusk light flooded the Karakoram Range. The Savage Mountain cast a lone shadow into the basin below. Atop the shadow, Messner saw himself – a minute silhouette over 20km away. 'It was the feeling of sitting on top of the world,' he remembers fondly. 'And it was the only time I ever had this feeling.'

Photos courtesy of the Messner Archive
@reinholdmessner_official // @hughfrancisanderson

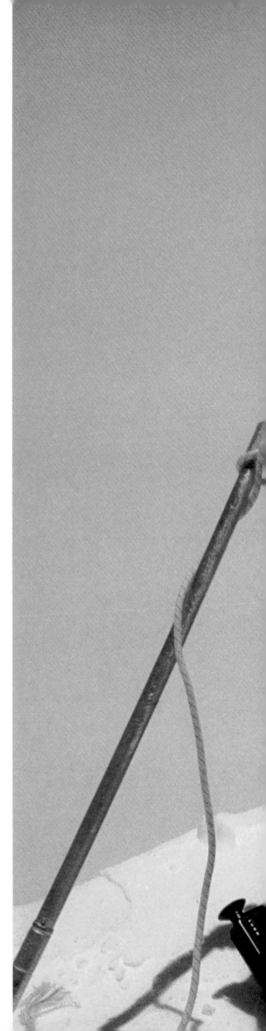

The Storm

Words: Louise Lenoble // Photo: Aidan Williams // Location: Switzerland

High in the Swiss Alps, on the summit of the Moléson, I feel the excitement rise within me even as the weather tips towards breaking point. I had not expected to find churning clouds and a bitter wind, but here I am on the line anyway, barefoot and ready. So I stand. Then the inevitable happens: the skies give way and the blizzard begins. Ahead, the highline stretches into whirling snowflakes.

The mind must be absolutely focused in order to walk on a 2.5cm ribbon of webbing between the clouds. The first step is always the hardest – the body only has seconds to adapt to the line's movements, and each limb must instantly synchronise and tune itself to the unpredictable shakes and vibrations. I reach within myself for the calmness, the serenity, required to navigate the wind and clouds ahead.

My arms reach for the skies and my feet instinctively shift into place as my eyes search for the far anchor. Disoriented by the wind-blown snowflakes blasting past in all directions, I momentarily feel that the world is upside down, that I can't rely on my vision anymore – unnerving in a situation where I must trust all of my senses. I can't help feeling cheated by the wind as it mauls my perception of gravity. But, deep in my flow state, I don't feel the cold. I've found the focus I need and I channel every scrap of mental energy into the challenge of balancing.

It feels doubly unreal because the conditions are so far from those I am used to. I began highlining in summer 2016 after seeing a guy in Strasbourg walking on a really big slackline – something that immediately sparked my curiosity. To me, slacklining was something practised on low 5cm-wide webbing, and at short lengths, but as soon as I saw this new style I had to find out more.

Today, slacklining drives my life. I'm in love with the feeling of freedom I experience when I'm on the line. All eventualities depend on me alone. Each step is an unconscious union of all my past experiences. I rely on myself, and I love the improvement that I feel from each attempt. The slackline culture, too, has pushed me to make decisions that have allowed me to explore my passions to the fullest.

In the beginning, it was so scary, and I found myself having to push my personal limits and leave my comfort zone like never before. But I discovered a mental strength within – something to which I'd previously been oblivious. This resilience didn't just come from fighting my fears, but also from teaching my brain to focus calmly and to keep my body moving in balance. I use this mental strength daily. It helps me to stay peaceful and focused through tough times, and allows me to feel more confident and able to manage my emotions.

Snowflakes roar past, but I am in balance. The cold does not move me. My bare feet enjoy the cosy feeling of being in the moment. This instant, right now, feels like a surreal mix of improbable factors coming together in harmony around my suspended bubble – a cocoon of focus and poise in the centre of the storm.

@louise_lenoble // @aidanwilliamsphoto

The Ridge

Words & Photo: **Andrew Terrill** // Location: **Italy**

The ridge stretched ahead, unmarred by trail or even a single scuffmark. Far below, thick beech forests grew. Down among the trees were wild boar, wolves, and Marsican brown bears, while up here were Apennine chamois; five crossed the airy crest directly ahead. This wasn't the Italy – or the Europe – that most people knew, but it was *exactly* the Europe I'd come to find. The quality of the wild was extraordinary. Undoubtedly, others walked here – I couldn't be the first – but I felt as though I were, and in appreciation I stepped lightly. Perhaps the next visitor would feel as much like an explorer as I did.

Following my map, I headed north along the ridge. Like most of the maps I'd used since leaving Calabria this map of the Abruzzo National Park lacked detail. Not that it mattered. The route ahead was obvious, and for several miles the ridge was broad and safe. There'd be no falling down mountains today. Four years earlier, I'd fallen 300m down a Swiss glacier. Somehow surviving, I'd looked at life anew, realising it was too precious to waste on full-time work. Instead, I'd chosen a different path, a life dedicated to long journeys on foot. But I never forgot the fall. It still haunted me.

Easy progress ceased a mile before the final summit. Unexpectedly, the ridge narrowed; two deep notches required the use of hands. The map had given no hint that difficulties lay ahead. Hesitantly, I pushed on. Since the fall I had struggled with exposure. Whenever slopes grew too steep the memory of falling came rushing back. In an attempt to overcome my fears I'd taken up rock climbing, but with a rope attached exposure was never so bad. The fear was worse when scrambling unroped; worse still when backpacking with a large rucksack. Clutching the ridge tightly, feeling top-heavy under my pack, I scrambled up 60-degree steps, worked over pinnacles, eased myself downwards above unnerving drops. My legs quivered, unsettled by the space beneath, and my breath came in shallow gasps. A lone chamois hissed at me from a ledge, perhaps afraid that I was a hunter. 'Don't worry, *Signore* Chamois,' I panted. 'I've other things on my mind.'

The ridge narrowed further, becoming a sharp-toothed spine of rock. Directly ahead, a tower blocked the way, and I approached it warily, fearful I'd have to retreat. But the limestone was solid, offering plentiful holds, and soon I was astride it, fear suddenly and inexplicably gone. In amazement I scrambled on, grinning with delight. For the first time in my life I felt completely at home in a situation where a single misstep would see me plummeting to my death. I didn't comprehend it, but celebrated it all the same. At the highest, spikiest, and most precarious perch I gave in to temptation and screamed at the top of my voice. The elation couldn't be suppressed.

The final stretch was easier. From the last summit I gazed back along the difficulties, enjoying a feeling of immense achievement. From here, the ridge looked oddly familiar, and the longer I stared the more I felt I'd been here before. Had I followed an identical ridge elsewhere, I wondered, scrambled over similar pinnacles on another walk? I was certain I hadn't. The déjà vu strengthened, and then I got it. The ridge was no longer just 'a ridge', no longer mere scenery to look at; it was a ridge I'd touched and had grown on; a ridge I now knew. It had become a part of who I now was.

This is an abridged extract from *The Earth Beneath My Feet*, the first of two books by Andrew Terrill about a 7,000-mile solo walk from Calabria to the top of Norway. The book reveals the wild side of Europe most people miss, and also explores the journey within – a passionate search for belonging within the natural world. @terrillonfoot

selkie

spirit

STORY & PHOTOGRAPHY: MIKE GUEST
WRITTEN BY: JENNY TOUGH
ADDITIONAL PHOTOGRAPHY: JO TENNANT // JAMES ROBERTSON
LOCATION: SCOTLAND

I'm looking back to the shore across a sea of glass. Hardly a breeze ripples the surface, and a tangerine sunrise fills the horizon, exhaling warmth onto the blue dawn – gorgeous light. The lights from street lamps are reflecting in the sea, and gulls glide silently overhead, scanning the coast for breakfast. As I peer through the viewfinder, the whole scene is effortless. I turn off my camera and float, alone in the sea for a bit. My physical surroundings are quiet, safe.

Still swirling in my mind is a powerful email from a friend that I read before heading out, pre-dawn this morning. A tragic loss and unexpected pain have entered his world. His gratitude – for the project I've started, and for my own candour on mental health through these early morning sessions – catches in my throat. My emotions are running high, but the world around me is peaceful and calm – uncharacteristic for this strip of Scottish coastline.

Just before I leave this quiet and safe space to head back to shore, where the day is starting for the rest of humanity, with all of its noise and movement, the seal gracefully bobs his head out, looking at me for a moment. I've seen him a few times on these morning shoots, but this time, as I smile at his wide black eyes, I wonder if he is my selkie.

The Celtic legend of selkies – 'seal folk' – tells of individuals who have two sides to them: their water-dwelling seal side, and their land-bound human side. I'd often wondered if perhaps I'm a bit like that. I spend so much of my time in the water, as a surfer and photographer, and sometimes I feel like I totally belong there. But then I return to land and walk around like a normal person, functioning in society. Without that selkie part, I'm not fully me. Not fully human.

I've been doing this every day since lockdown started. I get up at 3.00am, pull on my wetsuit, and take my camera down to the water. I paddle out to sea, then turn around and shoot the coming dawn. Although I'm mostly in the same place every day, it's always different. The weather changes; so does the light, the nature, the patterns in the water. There's always something that captures my interest, and I'm constantly being surprised. My wetsuit and surfboard are like my selkie costume, transforming me and adapting me to the water.

For two decades, I lived a fast-paced life of travel. When I had to return to my flat for the lockdown, it was the first time I had really been on my own in my home, and I quickly slipped into one of the darkest periods of my life. I had no idea how to deal with my brain. I had no idea what was going on.
 ▶ ▶

Photo: ©Jo Tennant

Another photographer and dear friend of mine said he had started shooting the dawn from the sea every morning – and, although he was all the way down in Cornwall where the sun rose much later, I decided to virtually join him. Dawn Days was born. What started as a simple commitment to go out in the water at the blue hour and shoot the dawn every single morning snowballed into a project that brings so many people together, and has become a wide conversation around mental health, providing a space for us guys to talk. The project was my lifeline. It gave me structure during that phase when the entire world seemed to have stopped, and the time I spent out in the water gave my mind that space to explore the dark corners.

While I'm out there in the mornings, thoughts and feelings come and go. I can choose to take notice of them or ignore them. I can prod them and try to understand them. Sometimes I am calm, and other mornings there is a lot going on. It's just like the place itself – on the calm mornings, I often see the wee seal, and wordlessly greet the graceful creature. But on some mornings, when I get up and look outside, the water doesn't look appealing. It's brown, turbulent, and the beach is being battered by howling easterlies. I never think it will be nice, but I convince myself to go out anyway. When I get out there and take my lens to a seal's-eye view, I manage to find something to focus on – maybe a street lamp, the rising sun, a bird. It's a creative challenge on those days, and it's an easy analogy for what sometimes goes on in our heads: sure, there is a storm all around you, but you can focus on one thing that excites you. Being out there on the dawn days helps me to concentrate on those small things – I can spend the whole morning focusing on the texture on the top of a wave, how it changes and moves.

I like building analogies with surfing. I've always been a surfer, so it helps me to make sense of things. I imagine the mind like a harbour. A lot of harbours only have one entrance, usually in the sheltered part. When the sea is raging outside and you need to get into that safe harbour, you have to be able to control the raging sea in order to get to the calm and peaceful haven. Many of the harbours on the Firth of Forth can only be accessed at high tide, so you've got to get in before the tide drops too far. I think about that when I'm feeling really low – like I'm in the middle of that harbour in the dark, in that shadowed part of myself. But I know the tide will come back in – it does so twice a day. Like the sun, the tide rises and falls. Some days I will feel low, but I will come back up. Knowing this helps to stop me from wallowing in it.

The seal dives again, effortlessly disappearing into his watery home, and I imagine that my selkie spirit is him. My other half – the human side of me – needs to return to land now. I can see the town of Portobello coming to life, lights flickering on in the apartment buildings and illuminating what was a strip of dark rectangles moments before. I'll have to dry off, get dressed, and go to work soon. I paddle smoothly to shore, and adapt my legs to upright walking again. I'm Mike now – until tomorrow.

Dawn Days is all about the act of immersing yourself in nature during the blue hour as you watch the dawn of the day. There are no rules: just be there, be present, and enjoy it.
@dawndays // @mr_guesty // @jprobertson // @jotennantphotographs

The Reindeer

Family

WORDS & PHOTOGRAPHY: PASCAL MANNAERTS
LOCATION: MONGOLIA

The day is setting over Tsagaan Nuur, a tiny, remote village beside Lake Khövsgöl in Mongolia, not far from the Russian border. The colourful roofs of the houses lined up along the lake shine like a rainbow under the golden rays of the setting sun. A cold wind suddenly rises, carrying a few clouds of dust and caressing us in an imperturbable silence. There is no-one around. It almost seems like this place has been abandoned by its inhabitants – a village at the end of the world. Here, time and space have taken on another dimension.

We have been in Tsagaan Nuur for two days, staying in a small wooden house just like the people who call this place home. To get here we travelled by jeep for three weeks across the country. Every night we slept in the yurts of nomads we met on the way. Already we feel far removed from our lives, and the world we know – but our journey is only beginning.

This evening, Bayrsaïhan joins us in our small house, accompanied by some friends living in the village. 'I am happy to guide you tomorrow through our mountains and forests to take you to see my family,' he tells me, smiling his broad smile. Bayrsaïhan is a member of the Tsaatan community. We met him yesterday, and were lucky to do so – he will only be in town for a few days before moving on to find his family. Purev, the young Mongolian accompanying us, obtained his contact before we left the capital Ulaanbaatar. Bayrsaïhan is tall, in his thirties, and incredibly elegant in his long red *deel*, the traditional Mongolian outfit, which he wears beautifully.

'We have a long day of riding ahead of us. Maybe two. Remember to pack everything you need, because once we leave Tsagaan Nuur you won't meet anyone until we reach the camp. Where we live, there are no other people except those of our community. No villages, no roads, no electricity, no place to get supplies.

'People call us Tsaatan, or Dukha,' he proudly tells us. 'We are one of the last groups of nomadic reindeer herders in the world. For thousands of years, we have been living with our reindeer in the middle of nature, on the remote steppes of Central Asia. We move regularly and only certain people know where to find us. I will guide you!'

Bayrsaïhan's good vibes are infectious and I can't help but show him how happy I am to have met him. 'You know, before leaving Europe, I thought it would be a dream to have the chance to meet the Tsaatan one day.' I wonder if he can see how important this moment is for me.

We share a few drinks. More than a few. The hours pass, punctuated by discussions on our experiences as first-time travellers in Mongolia – and also our laughter, especially when our new friends ask us to try on their traditional clothes, to see what we would look like in 'Mongolian version'. 'It suits you very well! You can stay and live with us now,' one of them says, sputtering with laughter. 'And since your nose is a bit long, you will be a very special Mongolian – everyone will want to know you.' Mongolia fascinates us, and I feel that this sincerely delights our guests. And for my part, looking ahead to the hoped-for encounter with the Tsaatan, I can't help thinking that the best of the trip is yet to come.

***

It's 5.30am. 'Good morning, everyone! I hope that waking up is not too hard this morning.' I am teasing my companions because, personally, I'm having a bit of a hard time getting started after yesterday's party. I fold up my sleeping bag and peek out the window. Rain is sluicing down. It looks like it has set in.

Food, suitable clothing, sleeping bags, first aid kit, fully charged batteries for the cameras – we finish packing our bags and loading them up onto the horses, hoping that we did not forget anything. We also have some extra food to offer the family. In remote areas where they live, supplies are always welcome.

At over 2,000m above sea level it's cool, very cool, and yet we are in the middle of June. A last warm cup of *süütei tsai* (traditional Mongolian tea) at the house, and the excitement of embarking on such an adventure, help us to lessen the shock when our feet sink deep into the cloying mud before even leaving the village. There are four of us: Bayrsaïhan, Robert (a Dutch friend who has been travelling with us in Mongolia since the beginning), Purev (our friend and Mongolian guide), and me. ▶ ▶

I soon learn that travelling through the taiga is not an easy thing. A morass of slippery mud coats every inch of the trail, and the horses struggle to move forward in the bog. It would be impossible for a human to venture here on foot. But Bayrsaïhan reassures us: 'Horses are used to it. In winter, it is even more difficult. We find ourselves in more than a metre of deep snow with our horses. If our horse has a problem on the way and cannot move forward, or if we get lost, the cold catches up with us very quickly and it becomes very dangerous. Some people never come back. But it's not winter now, so don't worry – I am sure you will come back to the village.' At that we all burst out laughing.

The coniferous forests we pass through feel like dark and sombre places as the vegetation grows more and more dense, and we each stay alert to avoid bumping into an unexpected branch and falling from our horse. I find the beauty of the surrounding nature breathtaking. To my Western gaze these landscapes exude an extreme solitude and a delicious mystery. Endless green vistas, so typical of Mongolia, suddenly reveal themselves through gaps in the trees. To experience such wonder is worth the rough ride. Little by little, we climb in altitude and the taiga gives way to immense snow-covered plateaus. We are now advancing in the snow. Suddenly, lightning

strikes a valley in the distance and our horses rear up, frightened by the thunderbolts.

The more the hours go by, the more I feel that we have left our world behind. I love this feeling of being lost and tiny before nature. In these moments, I always feel an incredible freedom – and, at the same time, a complete vulnerability. I think the combination of the two is interesting. It's total surrender. In such an environment, as human beings, we see our true worth to scale. It's good to come back to that awareness from time to time, adjusting our thoughts and feelings with humility towards nature. Nature rules.

But, for all the wonder, it would be truly impossible to find our way through these swamp forests without being accompanied by someone who knows the terrain. We have complete confidence in our benevolent guide with his indisputable charisma.

We advance in single file. My horse is always the last of the group. 'He's a lazy boy,' Bayrsaïhan says with a huge, unwavering smile. He reminds me that I can motivate my horse with 'tchoo, tchoo', a magic word commonly used in Mongolia to speed up horses. And, believe me, it works – at least sometimes. But not always for my 'lazy boy', who, unfortunately for me, must speak a different dialect.

The hours go by. Tiredness wins us over. The summer days are long, but this gives us hope that we can reach camp while it is still light, and in just one day of travel.   ▶ ▶

'Woooow! Look, here we are!' Bayrsaïhan suddenly whoops, and when I realise what this must mean my inner excitement climbs to new heights, warring with the fatigue. After more than 10 hours on the road, finally I can make out a few tiny white dots on the horizon. They are still far away but, yes, we can see the camp of the Tsaatan family.

A man and a woman watch us arrive: standing figures dwarfed by the immensity of the landscape stretching out in all directions. I later learn that they are Narahuu and his wife Bolorma. The colours of their clothes contrast with the endless green of the plains. Around them, their reindeer are resting peacefully – placid shapes occasionally munching at a tuft of grass or twitching an ear at a fly. I also see the silhouettes of children running around the tents. Everything around me seems to be happening in a slow-motion movie. As moments go, this one truly feels like a dream.

Bayrsaïhan comes first and finds Narahuu. We will later learn that they are cousins, and that Bayrsaïhan visits from time to time to bring food to them and to other Tsaatan families.

'Sain baina uu! [Hello!]'; 'Amar baina uu? [How are you?]' We shake hands with big smiles. Narahuu gives me a few friendly slaps on the back as if in welcome. The two youngest boys, introduced as Sosor and Tuvshinbayar, follow us close and never take their eyes off us. They seem so amused to see us among them.

We unload the horses and Bolorma takes us to their second tent, where we pile our luggage. This, Bolorma says by way of gesture and expression, is where we will sleep. Made primarily from birch bark, the Tsaatan's yurts superficially resemble the tepees of American Indigenous people, and inside we find hunting equipment, saddles, tools, and utensils – everything needed to survive in this elemental place. Afterwards, we all sit together to share a süütei tsai that Bolorma has prepared on the stove in the middle of the family tent. This hot beverage is welcome after all those long, cold hours on the road.

The members of the family don't speak English, but Bayrsaïhan and Purev play the interpreters. I am struck by how much communication is possible through simple looks and gestures. I can't help but stare at the mother, Bolorma, whose calm face exudes incredible kindness. Ulziisaihan and Ulziitsetseg, the two older daughters of Narahuu and Bolorma, also join us and sit by our side.

'I'm really happy to be here!' I blurt out impulsively, unable to resist telling them how happy I am right now. Bayrsaïhan translates with a smile, and then, after Narahuu speaks, translates his words back to us: 'We are happy to see you too! You have come a long way to reach us.' Narahuu offers us a few pieces of dried cheese (aaruul), typical of Mongolia.

This first contact with the family feels completely natural, and I find myself surprised at how moved I am by the sincerity of their welcome. In this country where we have been travelling for almost a month now, I have experienced so much spontaneity and hospitality – qualities of the people here that I have swiftly come to love. Even though we are complete strangers, we find ourselves welcomed in people's homes as if we were lifelong friends. Purev tells me that it is the way it happens in her country. This mutual aid, this hospitality, are essential components of Mongolia's nomadic culture.

The kids, especially the two youngest ones, have already adopted us. Sosor and Tuvshinbayar take us by the hand to see the reindeer, and, with gestures, they prompt us to caress them and give them hugs. They treat the reindeer with so much kindness and love, as if they were family members. The kids also show us how they play and sit on the reindeer, running, jumping, and landing on their backs – like cowboys, I think, but gently. The reindeer seem delighted. 'Well, I suggest that due to our fatigue from the long road, we try this instead tomorrow.' Robert agrees. The reindeer observe us curiously and sniff us up and down, as if to get used to us and validate our presence in their territory.

We've arrived in June, just after Narahuu and Bolorma's family have settled into their summer camp. Reindeer cannot handle heat well; during the warmer months they must be pastured at higher elevations. The family has moved here, to an altitude 2,300m, in open grasslands spread across the high steppes. It is just a perfect place for them to spend the summer. ▶▶

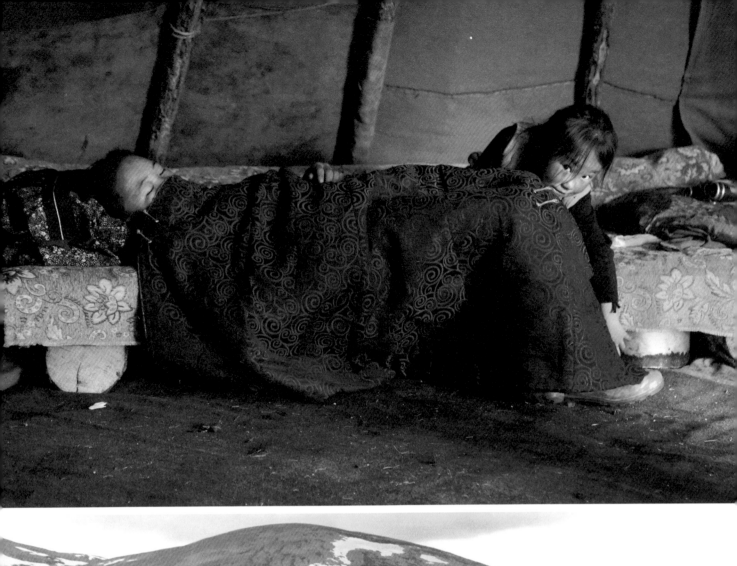

The reindeer and the Tsaatan people are totally dependent on one another. The Tsaatan depend on the reindeer for almost all of their basic needs: their reindeer provide them with milk, cheese, and transportation. They sew their clothes with reindeer hair, reindeer dung fuels their stoves, and their antlers are used to make tools. The reindeer are domesticated, and, in many ways, they are treated like family members and shown love and respect. Chores and activities revolve around the care and feeding of their reindeer. Herding tasks are shared amongst the camp, with children learning at a young age how to care for the animals and keep them safe.

***

Our time at the camp is now taking on a whole new rhythm. Family members are always keen to take us to learn about their day-to-day activities.

We find ourselves going with Narahuu across the plains on the backs of reindeer to collect wood for the evening fire. Every day, in late afternoon, Bolorma and her two daughters, Tuvshinbayar and Ulziisaihan, milk the reindeer – a ritual that seems fun to us when they suggest that we try to do it ourselves, all under the amused gaze of their two little brothers. 'You see, you're doing it better and better. I'm sure when you get home you'll want to have some reindeer at home,' Bolorma tells us while overseeing the operations, her words translated by a smirking Purev through the general laughter.

Moments of cooking and eating in the tent are fascinating, and always provide great opportunities for conversation about our very different lifestyles. Today Bolorma asks me if I have any pictures of my family with me. I show her some on my smartphone, as well as other pictures of my hometown, Brussels.

She speaks, and Bayrsaïhan, sitting nearby, recounts her story. 'I once visited the capital Ulaanbaatar. Life there in the city is not made for me. It completely frightened me. I would never think of leaving the plains and the mountains to lead a sedentary life, even though I know very well that life in the capital could be more comfortable.' She seems so peaceful saying that, and this simple question comes to my mind: 'Bolorma, can I ask you something? What makes you happy in life?' I see the emotion radiating from her face. Without hesitation, she answers frankly: 'My family and my reindeer. I do not need anything else. I am happy.'

Narahuu nods towards his wife, and adds a few words of his own: 'You know, Pascal – this is how it is for us, but with the younger generations, it's different. They are from another age, another era. They find themselves pinched between their desire for modernity and a sense of family loyalty. Many of them abandon the traditional way of life of their parents and prefer to turn to a sedentary life, in cities like Mörön or of course Ulaanbaatar. Only about 40 Tsaatan families continue the tradition today.'

▶▶

As Narahuu finishes, Bayrsaïhan spontaneously adds a few words of his own. 'I go back and forth regularly to Tsagaan Nuur or Mörön. It's an opportunity to look for supplies, but I'm also always happy to stay there for a bit. I have friends there. Life in the city offers things that I don't have if I live in the wilderness with the reindeer as the members of my community do. I like both – sometimes it's hard to choose. Maybe one day, too, I'll meet a girl in town. I might want to get married and have children there.'

'People are free. It is up to everyone's choice,' Narahuu concludes. 'But one thing is certain, our animals remain the centre of our universe, and here is where they feel their best.'

After almost a week spent together at the camp, we leave on horseback, as we arrived. We say goodbye with stars in our eyes, not knowing if we will ever meet each other again. 'Good luck during the rest of your trip in Mongolia and have a safe trip back home. Promise me one thing, that you will never forget those few days with us,' Narahuu tells me, as he adjusts my horse's saddle before I get on it. Bolorma gives each of us a reindeer head that Narahuu has carved with a knife from antlers. 'Keep this preciously – it will bring you happiness.' The children each give us a hug.

We hit the road on our horses. Mine is still the lazy boy of the gang, but this time I don't find it as annoying; his dithering allows me to turn back as many times as I want while I see our Tsaatan family getting smaller and smaller on the horizon. Every time they see me turning back to them they raise their hands to wave goodbye. I take a deep breath. All I can say to myself is *wow*.

There are adventures that seem to come out of a fairy tale or a childhood dream, where the magic of the experience transports you completely. There are experiences off the beaten track that challenge your conceptions and certainties, making you question your relationship to the world and nature. There are journeys and encounters that become treasures that you carry inside you forever. Our journey to meet the Tsaatan was all of these things.

@pascalmannaerts

Impact

Words: Hillary Allen // Photo: Guillem Casanova
Location: The Trømso Skyrace, Norway. August 2017

One misplaced step. The horizon turned upside down. I was airborne. I was falling off the edge of a cliff. I felt the first impact, then the second, then the third.

I hit the ground again and again and again. With each impact, I felt bones breaking, skin ripping. I grasped for something, anything, to stop my momentum, but I didn't know which way was up, and as soon as I hit the ground I was spinning and airborne once again. I heard my own voice, floating somewhere above my head, declaring to me, calmly, 'Hillary, this is it. You're dying.'

This was my death.

Relax.

You've got to relax. Breathe.

It will all be over soon.

I came to on the mountainside. The world was throbbing, pulsing in and out. I screamed out when the pain came, hoping that yelling would somehow release the intensity of the agony rushing over me. I felt like I was being suffocated. Unable to breathe or relax, I kicked my legs out of reflex and frustration. Then I thought to myself, *You're moving your legs; that's a good sign. You're not paralysed.* But then the pain would rush back. I shut my eyes tight, and flashes of red and yellow danced across my eyelids. It hurt so much I had to stop moving.

Somehow, I realised, I was only in my socks. My shoes must have flown off my feet somewhere along the way down the mountainside. I couldn't move my arms or hands, but tried to anyway. When I looked down, all I saw was a bundle of bones that didn't look like arms, and my wrists were turned the wrong way. There was so much blood. *What was happening?* I thought. *What had just happened?* I was confused, scared, and stranded – alone on the mountainside.

Suddenly there was a voice, and the face of another runner I vaguely recalled seeing earlier in the race. I had passed him as we ascended the steep part of the ridgeline, and we exchanged some words of encouragement. *Why was he here now? Had he fallen too?*

His arms were wrapped around me. His face was close to mine. *Had he been here the whole time?* He covered me with an emergency blanket – which was somehow still in the pack I was carrying – and later his jacket. He braced me and stayed with me, making sure I didn't fall any further down the mountainside.

Manu was his name, as I learned later. He had seen the rock fall, and me with it. Trained in first aid and wilderness responder training, Manu scrambled down the ridgeline after me.

Others had seen me fall too. My good friend Ian Corless, a professional photographer who worked for the Skyrunner World Series, was perched on the summit of the ridgeline waiting for my arrival, but as I came around the corner, what he saw through his lens wasn't what he expected. Another good friend, Martina Valmassoi, was with Ian. Martina, a professional ski mountaineer, runner, and photographer, was terrified when she saw me fall off the cliff. They both thought they had just witnessed my death. Panicked, they quickly called race director Kilian Jornet, who called the mountain rescue team. Martina, Ian, and Kilian scrambled their way down to me on the side of the mountain.

As I lay there, seeing the fear in their eyes, their features expressed what I was already thinking: *I'm dying.*

Martina put her puffy jacket over me, mostly to cover the blood but also to keep me warm. My body convulsed, either from pain, loss of blood, or shock – I couldn't tell which. I focused on Martina's voice as she stroked my head and told me it would all be OK.

After an agonising 30 minutes, I heard the bellowing sound of the helicopter. A doctor lowered onto the ridgeline and scrambled down to me to assess the damage. 'Inhale,' he told me as he sprayed something up my nose, some sort of painkiller. It dulled the pain, but not my confusion. My eyes took in the shapes of their faces... they were still full of fear.

From that point on things moved quickly. There was a lot of movement. There was a lot of pain. Ian, Kilian, Manu, Martina, and the doctor tried to stabilise me. They shuffled rocks around, trying to make room to hoist me up onto the cot. The agony was unbearable. With every movement, I yelled out in anguish, my cries eventually dissipating into a whisper. I didn't know where the pain was exactly. I couldn't pinpoint it or figure out where it originated from – I felt it all over. As I was secured to the cot, the doctor fastened himself by my side and signalled to the helicopter pilot, who flew upward and outward from the side of Hamperokken Ridge. The feeling of falling swept over me again, and I closed my eyes tight.

Breathe. It will all be over soon.

In 2017, world-class ultrarunner Hillary Allen was at the top of her sport, and racing near the front of Norway's 50km Tromsø Skyrace when she fell 150ft off an exposed ridge, breaking two ribs, fracturing her back, rupturing a ligament in her foot, and breaking both wrists.

The full story of her recovery and fight to return to the life she loves is told in her book *Out and Back: A Runner's Story of Survival and Recovery Against All Odds.*
@hillygoat_climbs // @guillem_casanova

The Catch

Words & Photo: Alex Krowiak // Location: Sea of Cortez

It would be ridiculous to suggest that ours was anything but a makeshift expedition. It's early morning on the third day travelling along the coast of the Sea of Cortez, following a loosely sketched map and our guidebook – a tattered and dog-eared copy of John Steinbeck's *The Log from the Sea of Cortez*. The shifting tones of the rising sun illuminate a land where barren desert mountains fall into a sea lush with life. For centuries, the drama of the landscape here has attracted explorers. It is what called John Steinbeck to sail through the many coves of this coastline 80 years ago. And it is what we seek on our expedition, in the hope of capturing images to document it.

Like Steinbeck and his team, our goal is to explore the protean life of the region's tide pools – the dancing bristle stars, scuttling Sally Lightfoot crabs, and otherworldly octopuses whose environments shift by the minute as the tide ebbs and flows. We begin to comb the beaches and overturn rocks for signs of life with one question in mind: how has the region changed in the 80 years since Steinbeck was here? Situated 100 miles from the burgeoning development of Cabo, this morning's site is particularly isolated. On the horizon, a lone sailboat gently drifts past the untouched islands of the Sea of Cortez. Behind us, fishermen from a small community ready their vessels for a day on the water, no doubt dreaming of full nets and full stomachs – an anachronism in a world of ever-increasing commercial fishing and coastline development. There's a purity here that we haven't experienced on our trip until now.

Soon, loud splashes interrupt the gently lapping waves. We quickly glance up towards the source and see a spear fisherman emerging from the shallows: a neoprene-clad figure with a broad rubber belt buckled around his waist. His gear is tucked under his arms as he delicately traverses the slippery boulders of the tide pools. Curious about his catch, we approach him and begin to chat. His collection bag is brimming with *pulpos* – octopuses freshly collected from the rocky crevices just beneath our feet. Together, the pulpos create a squirming mass that bulges from the mesh of the bag. As we begin to speak with him, Jesús shows us scattered empty shells arranged in a rough circle – the remnants of an octopus's meal, and the signifier of where to search. He points to the horizon, names the many islands, and tells us which are his favourite to hunt from. It's clear that his connection to the environment here runs deeper than we can imagine. We ask about change, about what Jesús has seen over his time in the water here. He replies simply: *'Igual que siempre.'* Same as ever. For us, viewing from an outside perspective, this is a return to what Steinbeck saw – a rugged version of the Baja, untouched and teeming with life. For Jesús, it's his daily endeavour. His existence.

The conversation is abruptly cut short as he spots another catch. With a swift and subtle movement, he reaches into the water and emerges with eight limbs dangling from his gloved hand. We watch in amazement as the octopus crawls up the length of his arm, its defensive skin cells flashing a firework show of colour, still dripping with the ink it ejected as a last resort. Jesús places it into the mesh bag with the others before turning towards his home, ready to feed his family.

@alex_krowiak

Entelechy

Words: Becki Vale // Photo: Tom McNally // Location: England

I have always felt an affinity for cold environments, deeply appreciating not just the allure and potential of nature's frozen architecture but how close they can take you to experiencing what it truly feels like to survive. Winter commands your respect and tolerates your presence on its terms.

This mountain pool, elevated some 200m above sea level, is hidden in a hanging valley at the epicentre of the Lakeland fells. I spent the journey here reading clues in the steepening landscape – telltale signs of whether or not I would find ice, the winterscape revealing impressions in the powder of visitors long gone. However, just a few steps off the main path I find that, this evening, I am the first to fracture the frozen lances of grass. As I pad closer with my bare feet, the sight of the crusted pane atop the tarn fills me with rapture. My eyes soften as I admire the delicacy with which it stretches to meet the undulations of the shore. Its soft opacity reflects the golden hues of the setting sun.

Cold curiosity didn't begin here for me. It grew from a fascination, fostered in sterile laboratories, as I fathomed how extreme environments – sub-zero or otherwise – interplay with human physiology. The ways we instinctively attempt to cope with such exposure led me to crave 'how' long before the first-hand thrill of immersion. But, in truth, my preparedness for this swim didn't really start there. Our aquatic past has left us with inherent responses to natural stressors like cold water.

The slapping of the axe and eerie creaking of the shards as they slip beneath the sheet could feel destructive, but everything about this frozen moment is temporary. Water's ability to constantly shapeshift is complemented by winter's power to reset the world to pristine overnight.

The channel is complete: a sliver of the inky depth exposed. The scene of the weapon-wielding warrior is juxtaposed with feelings of raw vulnerability as I set the axe down on the shore and face the cold, disarmed. Subconsciously tapping into atavistic reflexes that literature and apparatus tell me are there, my anticipation gives way to a calming trust.

The water slowly engulfs me, viscous, on the brink of metamorphosis. A visceral flooding of the senses elates and cleanses. My heart rate settles as my body remembers how to equilibrate from aeons of learning. Survival instinct eradicates superfluous musings. Inside and out everything is silent, everything is real. In those minutes I experience a timeless existence, nothing separating me from those that have come before. My body reminds me not to overstay my welcome. Afloat, I turn, protecting soft, anaesthetised skin from razor-sharp edges and fragments as I gravitate towards the bank. I find my footing and stand. The cold peels down me. Fire now kisses skin moments ago numbed by a glacial grasp. Lifted by the intensity of both these feelings, I rise, galvanised, with a fierce sense of belonging.

My inner academic wants to label the processes taking place beneath the surface in this quest for ice, but am I purely fulfilling a physical need? Chasing the chemical rush? Or is there more to this than science and psychology can explain: the realisation of ancient potential confirming that I am, in this moment, exactly where I belong?

@beckivale // @intotheoutside // @tommcnallyphotography

A SINGLE MOMENT

Through the

RAGN

STORY & PHOTOGRAPHY: ALBERTO OJEMBARRENA
LOCATION: ICELAND

ARÖK

Fires

Norse mythology speaks of the Ragnarök, the battle of the end of the world between the Norse gods and the giants. But, as with most myths, it was inspired by real stories and natural phenomena.

This is the tale of an invisible route through a landscape that seemed deeply hostile, its roots entwined with the old legends of Iceland and the Norse settlers.

I looked back and saw my footprints in the wet black sand of the mountain, tailing down the slope we had just laboriously climbed. I looked forward, shielding my eyes with a hand against the blowing rain, and tried to visualise our destination for the day. Warm sweat mixed with the cold raindrops blatting against my jacket. For two days we had been hiking the vast landscapes of the Icelandic Highlands and a huge storm was about to arrive. I could just make out the next hut on the distant horizon, a small wooden cabin framed by yellow mossy hills receding into the mist.

Monica and I started the weary descent towards the valley. My backpack was feeling heavier that evening, maybe because of the strain of hiking for hours in the fog, wind, and rain. A few metres in front, Monica – a figure in red Gore-Tex – was trying to scout out the near-invisible path leading us to the hut. Her leather boots, worn out after so many hikes in the most remote areas of Iceland year after year, struck a steady and confident rhythm as she followed the path's thread through the valley. Perhaps sensing me watching her, she stopped and looked back to me. Her smile was small but vigorous. 'C'mon! We are almost there!' she shouted, trying to raise her voice over the increasing wind.

After her words faded, the only sounds across the valley were our footsteps, our heavy breathing, and the cold gusts whispering over the peaks of the nearby mountains.

We could see the hut in the distance, but it was like a mirage. Every time I calculated the distance left it was as if we hadn't walked at all. Finally, after hours of worsening weather, we found ourselves in front of the old wooden door – wet and tired, but both smiling. Monica and I had waited for an adventure like this for months. Finally we were living it.

Grateful to reach shelter at last, I dumped my backpack on the cold stone floor at the entrance, stretched – I could feel every mile – and got ready to light the paraffin stove, completely black after so many years warming the nights for farmers and hikers who ventured into these forgotten lands. The hut was freezing. Slowly, as the stove worked its magic, the small room turned into a warm and cosy space. Monica started boiling some water for our mandatory post-hike teas and we squeezed onto a bench as close to the stove as we could. I rubbed my hands to warm them while Monica raised her phone and waved it above her head, trying to find some signal, then squinted at the screen. 'Any news?' I asked her. 'I wish! We are too deep in the valley. I guess there will be nothing until higher ground tomorrow.'

Unspoken between us was one simple fact: we knew that the real cold was coming. In a few days a big storm was going to arrive. Even at that moment, after two cups of that spicy tea that we always liked to carry with us, we couldn't bring ourselves to remove our beanies and down jackets. ▸▸

But in Iceland there is never a perfect time for hiking in perfect conditions. Sometimes you just have to grab opportunities if you feel that there's the slightest chance.

***

Before we began our hike into that unbeaten landscape, Monica and I had been wardening at the Landmannalaugar Hut. Every day for the last month of that summer I had woken surrounded by lava fields and rhyolite mountains. Every day I had brewed black coffee, opened up our small information centre, and started to welcome the new hikers arriving to take on the famous Laugavegur Trail. If not taking care of jobs around the office, I'd be found hiking to the tops of the surrounding mountains, always looking in the opposite direction to the crowded trails heading south.

At the end of the season, the weather was growing stormier by the day. Just a few travellers dared to come at the end of September to the Icelandic Highlands, and Monica and I were meant to leave with the last bus. But that evening everything changed.

Monica had been pouring hot water for a cup of tea. 'So that's it? We leave in a few days?'

Neither of us was sure of wanting to return to the capital. We had enjoyed a summer filled with amazing experiences and new friendships, but we had missed the chance of hiking one last time before access was closed. That was when a strong fist knocked on the door, and less than a second after that a friendly face appeared behind it. Soaking wet in his hand-made wool sweater, Klemmi entered the room smiling broadly under his moustache. '*Focking geggjað!* [fucking crazy!]' he exclaimed while wringing out his beanie.

He had been driving the whole morning to Landmannalaugar under the hard rain, and the following day he would drive further east for what in Iceland we call *trúss* – delivering food boxes and luggage for hiking groups. The Icelandic Highlands are known for the famous Laugavegur Trail, but there are smaller, remoter trails connecting every corner of the land. Most are almost invisible: unmarked trace paths followed only by sheep and farmers. Klemmi was one of the few who knew about the start of these trails. We were definitely not expecting to find him that day, and with a small window of good weather before a huge storm, we decided to enquire about one last adventure.

'Have you seen the forecast?' he said. But, after a long talk about the weather and the trails, he agreed to take us to one of the most remote places you can get to in the southern Icelandic Highlands: Langisjór Lake. From there we hoped to begin one last hike before the summer was over. It was a gamble, but it would be our last chance. And sometimes the best stories begin with a dash of uncertainty, even jeopardy – just like the Norse legends that underpin this landscape.

***

That night at the remote cabin, as I lay inside my sleeping bag with the aroma of burning paraffin from the blackened stove in my nostrils, a thought came to my mind: *This is it. There's no return now.*

***

It had been cold overnight; I woke to find condensation on my sleeping bag. After a hot breakfast, I turned off the stove and, when Monica opened the door, colder air swirled in to disperse the lingering breakfast smells. The thick fog was gone. Instead, muted grey clouds and drizzle revealed the most bewitching sight, beautiful yet also unnerving: a lava forest, crowding around the hut as if it had sprung up overnight. Enormous irregular pillars of volcanic rock rose two or three metres from the ground all around us. Tufts of white and grey lichens sprouted from these monoliths, and with their crowns of green moss and other vegetation they looked like the trunks of some ancient forest. Some of the pillars were grouped in small formations; others

▷▷

76

stood by themselves in the middle of the field, like vestiges of a lost battle. It was exactly as I had pictured in my head when I read about the mythology of the area we were about to hike. The entrance to this forgotten land was guarded by a herd of petrified *trölls*.

The encounter both enthralled and slightly unsettled us. After packing our rucksacks, we set out in silence, hiking towards a steep hill, and found ourselves suddenly in a vast area with nothing to guide us – no marked trails, no landmarks, nothing at all. Monica took her GPS out of her pocket. She had always been confident with navigation in the mountains, but this time she was quieter than usual, and she looked around a couple of times, trying to get some reference points. She looked back to the GPS, and after a few seconds of meditating her decision she put the device away again. 'This way, c'mon,' she said, and her tone inspired confidence. I followed her lead.

Slowly, the landscape changed – from brown soil and low bushes to black rock, veined deeply where once water had flowed, and peppered by the vivid colours of green moss and red tones that appeared more and more frequently. Then we reached the edge of a black cliff, and immediately we knew where we were. It was unmistakable.

Eldgjá ('fire gorge'), 40km long, is the biggest volcanic canyon in the world – the place whose eruption is said to have inspired the Ragnarök legend. In front of us was a huge fissure, rent in the mythic past by the eruption of the volcanic system linking the Katla and Eldgjá volcanoes: proof for the old settlers of that legendary battle. We tried to find the canyon's end on the horizon, but could not see it. I pictured myself in the middle of that massive lava flood, standing on the edge of the gates of hell, feeling the rage of the pagan gods.

We descended into the ravine. Reddish and green hues created a sense of drama and magic, accentuated by the stormy clouds churning above the fissure. Huge boulders stood in the middle of the valley, broken from the top volcanic tephra layers long ago, as if dropped there by supernatural creatures.

After several kilometres in this dry fissure, the atmosphere began to feel heavy, humid, and I could hear a soft murmur gradually growing louder until it rose up through the ground into our boots – a deep, irresistible vibration. Suddenly we found ourselves facing Ófærufoss: a massive seething spout of water falling from the top of the tephra cliffs, forcing its way between the black rocks and mossy walls of the valley. After a few minutes gazing at the waterfall, completely mesmerised, we started to follow the course of the widening river. The boulders gained a tenuous clothing of green moss as we walked. After every cataclysmic battle of the old gods, nature found its way again.

***

Before the storm came the pause. The peace before the Ragnarök.

After a couple of hours listening to the wind beat against the walls of our hut, the weather slowly abated and the black clouds on the horizon stopped their advance. A shy sliver of light opened in the distance for a moment. It was a false omen.

We tried to use the old radio to communicate with Kristín, waiting for us in a hut further down the trail, but it seemed useless; there was no chance of letting her know that we were coming the following day. Old maps from the Geodetic Institute lay in a pile on one shelf. I studied them for a couple of hours with a cup of ground coffee that I had found in a jar. The sweet aroma mixed with the wet smell from our clothes and boots drying near the stove, but finally we felt warm. Monica checked her GPS; even though we knew that we were so close to the following hut, where Kristín was waiting for us, we had no doubt that the next day was going to be gruelling.

Pensively, Monica looked out of the window at the shaft of sunlight playing through a gap in the clouds. 'Maybe the weather will change after all.'

▶ ▶

I smiled back at her and poured more Icelandic *kaffi* into my mug. I looked again through the grimy panes, shivering from the breeze filtering through the window's joints. 'No, I wouldn't say so,' I said while sipping my coffee. I truly could feel it – like the old wives' tale, I could feel the storm in my bones, and I felt conflicted between excitement and concern as the two forces warred within me. This pause in the weather before the storm just made me feel nervous. The thing about tension is that it inevitably breaks.

The next stage would be committing. I looked at Monica and exhaled deeply, wondering if she could see the complex blend of worry and excitement I felt. She looked back at me. Did she feel the same? Later, while we were eating, a fusillade of rain suddenly began hammering against the hut's roof – hard rain, intensifying hour after hour. I slipped into my sleeping bag and tossed and turned on the plastic mattress for hours, brooding on the upcoming challenge.

***

'Only fifteen kilometres!' Monica shouted over the blowing wind. The rain had been intense from the moment we had stepped outside the hut that morning.

We climbed up through a black tephra canyon and into a desert of sediment left behind by ancient glaciers. I looked back one last time. In the distance were flashes of blue sky, but we were heading in the opposite direction and my boots were sinking into a grey mire churned up by the rain. Plummeting temperatures last night had frozen the valley sides, and we tried to thread a weaving route between the firmer areas, desperately trying to avoid sinking into the mud. Some valleys harboured old wreaths of firm snow – or at least they looked firm until we stepped onto them and sank deep into collapsing slush, slowing our progress even further. The weather gave us no truce. Gale-force winds continually pushed us off course, and we were so soaked that it seemed pointless to take off boots before fording rivers. *Splash, squelch, splash* was the soundtrack to our hike – head down, hood turned against the shrieking storm, eyes focused on the little patch of ground right at our feet.

And then we heard it, like the hoofbeats of horses arriving on the battlefield, a ferocious surge of rain and hail bearing down on us. I looked up at Monica. She was stumbling wearily and I grabbed her hand. Her mitten was completely saturated. Her hood drooped down towards the ground, water spattering from its brim, and I could hardly see her face. 'I'm fine, no worries,' she murmured. 'We are close. We should keep going.' I felt as exhausted as she looked, but she was right. If we stopped now we might not get going again.

Hard hours later, I finally caught sight of the hut: a tenuous ghost of a building floating in and out of vision a few hundred metres away. As we neared, the mirage solidified and I dared to believe that we'd reached our destination. That we had made it through the storm. Monica, still just ahead of me, was visibly shaking as she staggered forward, but I heard her let out a happy sigh of relief. I exhaled too. How much further could either of us have gone in those conditions? I couldn't even feel my hands, and every layer of clothing was soaked through to the skin. Raindrops dripped from my beard and the hair in front of my eyes.

As we drew closer, a familiar face appeared framed in the doorway. Kristín's long blonde hair was unmistakable, even from this distance, and I felt something in me unknot as I realised

that we'd reached safety, we'd come through the fires. She pulled on a Gore-Tex jacket and came running and screaming in joy to us. Later that evening, Kristín told us that an Orange Alert had been announced because of the extreme weather in the Highlands. 'I was waiting for you to radio from another hut,' she told us, and despite the smiles and the defused tension I saw an echo of anxiety in her eyes. 'I'm so happy that you are finally through. It must have been a battle.'

***

For the last three days of our journey, we connected from Hvanngil to the Álftavatn lake, joining the last stages of the Laugavegur Trail to Thórsmörk. The weather finally gave us a break. Storm and darkness gave way to quiet views and beautiful sunsets, and we ended our trip with one of the best days I'd ever had in Iceland. The warm atmosphere of Langidalur's surroundings is something I can never tire of: the bright birch trees, the Eyjafjallajökull glacier glinting in the distance, the land of the gods, and the feeling of journeying through a place where everything around you is more alive than yourself. Yet, much as I enjoyed the more peaceful end to our hike, nothing stands out in my memory more vividly than those days of drama in the untrodden volcanic hinterlands, where the stories of old seemed to follow every step.

@amarokadventures // amarok.is // @albertooutdoors // @moka_guide

UNTI

WORDS: ANNA VON BOETTICHER
PHOTOGRAPHY: TOBIAS FRIEDRICH
LOCATION: GREENLAND

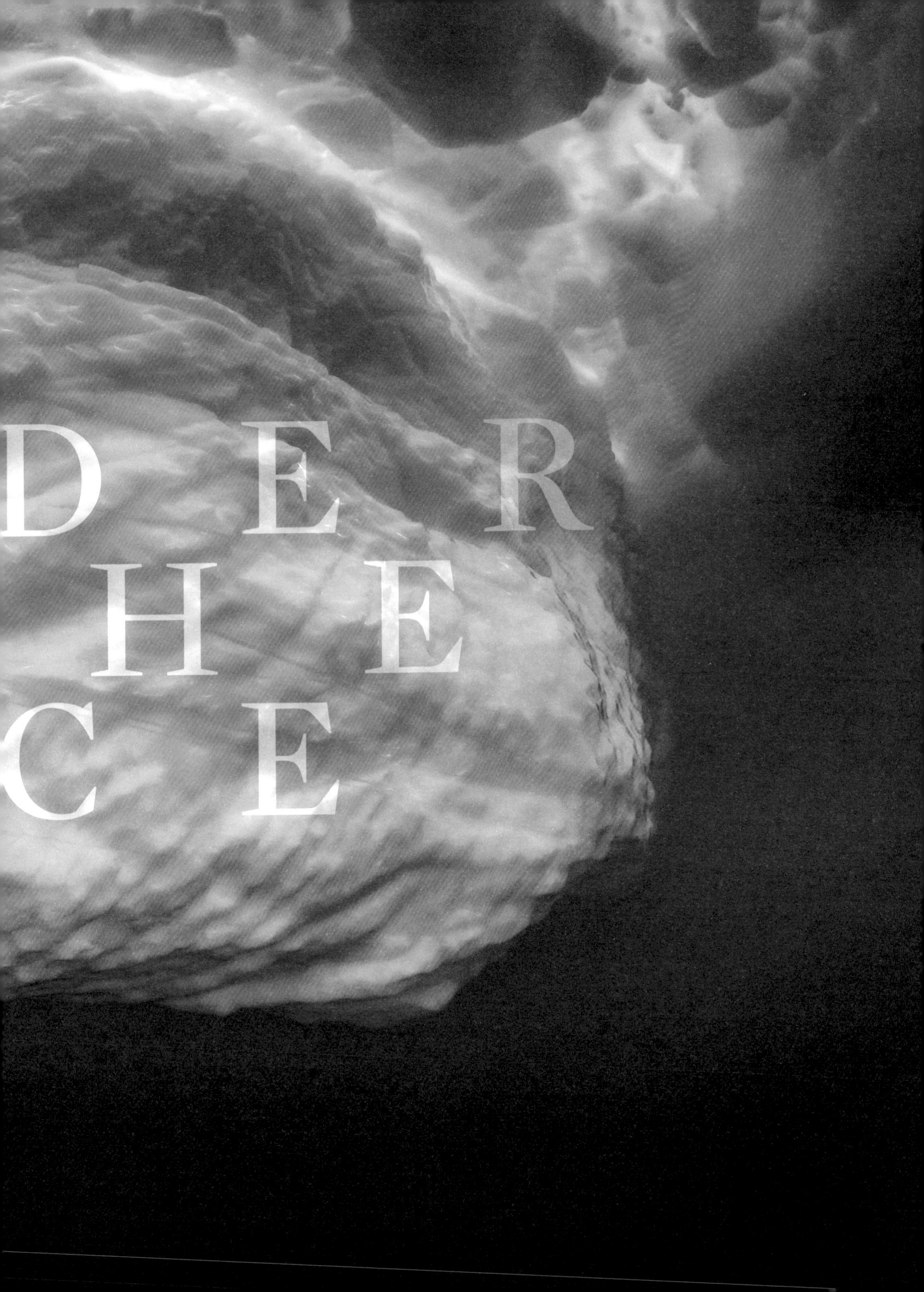
DER
HE
CE

'I saw mesmerising shapes formed hundreds of years ago, with ice so old and clear it shimmered turquoise when everything around receded into shades of black and white.'

At times, being a freediver means answering many questions. 'How deep did you go?' people want to know, and: 'did you see anything?' To most, what I do only makes sense if there is something in it, something worthwhile. To me, being there is enough and, to me, there are always things to discover.

What did I see?

I saw the light of the deep. One hundred metres below in the Mediterranean Sea, I saw it turn to near-black in the nothingness beneath me. On my way up from a record dive, I saw a visible layer of warmer water extend into the distance, like a cloudy sky fading to an endless horizon – a sight that made me pause and simply wonder. I watched a tiny crab climb onto my hand out in the open ocean, far from land, and I saw a huge orca come close to take a look at me in the dark waters of the Norwegian polar night. Under the thick ice of a frozen fjord in Greenland, I saw an alien world that seems unknowable to us, yet is linked to our lives in ways we struggle to understand. This is the story I want to tell: the story of the Arctic ice. As you read, and you imagine the burning desire to breathe, and think *how awful* and *I could never*, I hope to take you beyond the instinctive fear to show you the beauty of a place unseen by human eyes. A beauty that must be earned.

On our first morning we woke to a sky heavy with snow, the air so cold it attacked our faces with sharp teeth as we made our way down to the shore through the colourful village of Tasiilaq. With a population of fewer than 2,000 people, it is the largest settlement on the otherwise wild and empty coast of East Greenland. The long fins I carried under my arm drew curious looks from the locals, who were used to visitors coming for dog-sledding excursions rather than a freediver trying to explore a freezing sea. People associate diving with silence, but the sounds of each new environment stick in my mind. I can still hear the ice crunch with our steps. It resonated under the sleds we used to transport our gear, and, as the tide shifted, it filled the air with a terrifying boom that had me looking for the crack that must surely be opening below my feet. For me, the ring of the large saw biting into the frozen surface as we cut our triangular holes is forever tied to the fjord that lay beneath us: 200m of water, dark and still.

Ice covers the fjord of Tasiilaq for close to half of the year, with icebergs that have drifted into the bay over the summer frozen in place like boulders dumped in a valley by an ancient glacier. We selected what looked like a promising iceberg, and prepared our holes right next to it. There were six of us, diving in pairs. Everyone was using scuba equipment except me – as a freediver, I would take nothing but a single breath. Professional underwater photographer Tobias Friedrich and I decided to start out together on this morning, a step that would turn into a working relationship built on friendship and trust.

As I slipped my fins into the black water, at –3 degrees C colder than any I had experienced so far, I had my first taste of the brutal conditions we had come to explore. Salt water can drop to below zero under the ice and every degree colder is an extreme experience in itself. Slowing the

▶▶

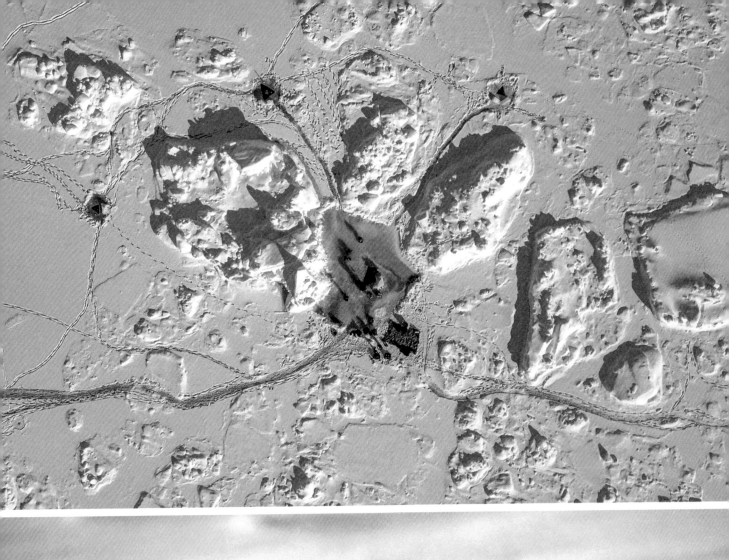

'Down below in the cold water, my heartbeat slowed
and my mind opened to the harsh beauty around me,
and there, finally, the spinning thoughts stilled and
I felt myself again.'

breath that flowed into my lungs, I closed my eyes and let myself sense my surroundings. The air freezing my fingers through the neoprene gloves. The feel of the sea, chilling my core. I separated my mind from the intense cold, took a final, deep breath, and drove my body through the small hole in one smooth motion. One kick. Two kicks. And then, I looked.

First, there was nothing but the inky darkness of the fjord below, drawing me down. But then, as I lifted my eyes, I saw a stark, monochrome universe of light and shadow, of water and ice. I saw mesmerising shapes formed hundreds of years ago, with ice so old and clear it shimmered turquoise when everything around receded into shades of black and white. I saw a world of icebergs; some perfectly round, some full of angles and corners. I saw them shine silver close to the surface, darkening underneath to charcoal-black as they reflected the shadows of the deep. I saw canyons I would swim through and holes that made me want to explore, but for a moment I simply hung there, holding on to the safety line, motionless and stunned.

I had come to Greenland looking for a unique experience as a freediver, but also longing for the peace we can find in nature. After the sudden death of my mother, life had been nothing but turmoil, with no room to grieve. I hadn't slept in months. Now, I stood on the frozen fjord, staring at the landscape and the sky, and felt the true, inescapable sadness sink in: a sadness I had wanted to give room to. Down below in the cold water, my heartbeat slowed and my mind opened to the harsh beauty around me, and there, finally, the spinning thoughts stilled and I felt myself again. I knew then that I had come to the right place – one I had wished to see since I was a child dreaming of adventures in the wild.

Every night, after long hours exposed to the Arctic, I sank into a deep, restful sleep. Day after day, we returned to the ice. The wind drove the snow across the landscape and chilled the air to -27 degrees C as we battled the conditions. In a matter of minutes slush would form in the holes we had cut. As soon as I surfaced to breathe, the water on my face turned to a glaze of ice, while the sharp wind forced my body temperature down even more than the freezing water. This left me no choice but to minimise the time I spent recovering, and made the dives more challenging still. All of it, to me, was sheer joy.

We soon came to realise that I could not swim around the icebergs while tethered to the line without getting tangled, and so, after careful planning, decided to take the risk to go without it. It worked beautifully, until the inevitable happened: I got lost.

Tobias and I were exploring the largest iceberg we had found so far. He had dived to around 25m and swum 40m away in order to take a shot wide enough to capture its scale with me in it. As I dropped down from our small hole, I let myself sink beyond the berg's flat bottom. The darkness underneath me seemed to extend into space, making me feel suspended on the edge of the world while I listened to the faint whisper of waves lifting the frozen surface above my head. I lingered below the iceberg, turning this way and that to look in all directions, vaguely aware of Tobias in the distance, before slowly making my way back up. Soon it would be time to breathe, but for now I was fascinated by the strange world around me.

The moment I realised I was in trouble came when I reached around 5m depth and expected to be near the welcoming doorway to my next breath. I saw many spots of light, but none of them was my hole. I knew then that I was truly lost, with no way to easily find the exit. *Well, this is an entirely new level of problem*, I thought.

▶ ▶

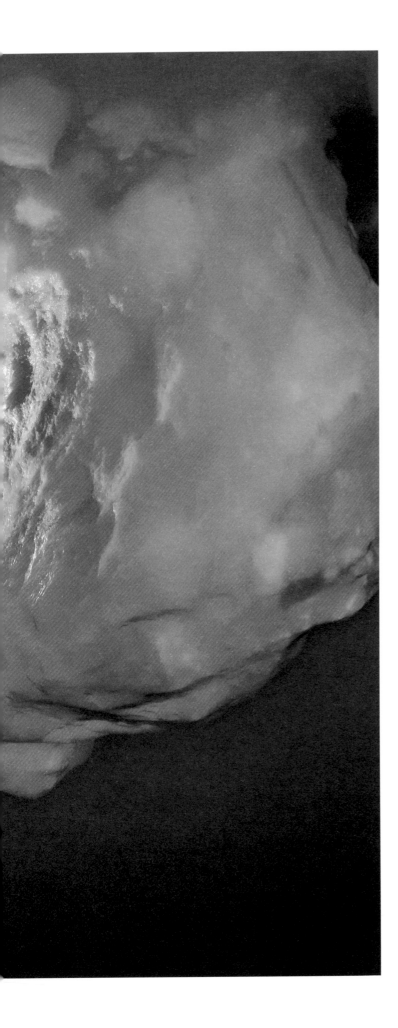

Panic is the single thing that could have ended my life at this point. Had I started to swim around, hard and fast, looking for an escape, I would most likely have gone deeper under the ice and further away from the hole while rapidly burning through my body's last reserves of oxygen. Had Tobias tried to go after me, he too would have lost his way. No-one could have helped us then. No-one could have found us. These dives were on the edge of what is manageable in this environment, and they were possible only because I knew, before I even set foot there, that when things go wrong I am able to respond calmly. I saved the fear for later and switched to solving my problem.

With no hope of finding the exit from my location, I decided that my only chance was to drop back down. I needed to gain a broader overview of the surface to increase my chances of spotting the triangular hole silhouetted against the light. As I turned, against every natural instinct, to swim away from the air above, I saw Tobias close by, pointing. He had kept his eye on me after taking his picture from afar, seen me lost, and swum quickly over to guide me back. I could not easily have taken air from him – scuba gear is already challenged by freezing in these conditions, and it would have put us both at risk. But he was there when it counted. I knew I could rely on him, and he on me. Back on the surface, as I took my first breath, I was full of joy at what I had just seen under the ice, and proud of the team we had become.

We adjusted our system with added markers for me to spot underwater and continued to explore, safely, for the rest of our time there. Every dive we did in that environment was a challenge, every hour we spent out there cold and tough. Yet what remains etched into my mind is not the discomfort or the risk. As I exposed myself to the alien universe under the ice, I felt – more than anything – that we cannot separate ourselves from any part of this world, no matter how distant it seems to be from our daily lives.

How deep did I go? How long did I stay? I don't know. Does it matter? I saw the world below the surface, and it filled me with wonder.

the

plumb

WORDS: TOM HILL
PHOTOGRAPHY: DUNCAN PHILPOTT & SAM NEEDHAM // ORBEA
LOCATION: GUNNERSIDE, UK

line

Each stamp on the door of the Old Working Smithy represents a single moment in time. The crisp edges left by the branding iron may have been dulled by two centuries of Yorkshire weather, but most are still legible: a tactile connection to the history of Swaledale. On this early spring day, the light catches the grain of the wood, creating valleys and ridges reminiscent of the dales in which we've spent the day riding. As we step inside, the low watery sun streams through the open doorway over uneven flagstones, stretching to the back of the smithy.

In the early 1800s, Stephen Calvert's great-great-great-great-grandfather would have stood where Stephen is standing now, working the bellows and bringing the furnace up to temperature. Once the metal was glowing hot, his clogged feet would have shuffled around 180 degrees before he shaped the pliable iron one hammer strike at a time. More than 200 years later, standing in that battered doorway of the smithy in Gunnerside, we watch Stephen replicate the process taught to him by his father and grandfather. Light filters through the dust and cracks of the tiny windowpanes, casting shadows into the cluttered corners of the room. Modern footwear has replaced the clogs of centuries past, but a square of wood on the stone floor remains, worn into a shallow hollow by the generations of Calverts moving back and forth between the furnace and anvil.

The rhythmic ringing of metal on metal contrasts with earlier that day when we looked down the deep V-shaped valley of Gunnerside Gill. Mist and rain rolled in and out like the tide as we rode across the bleak moorland. The only noise came from an occasional startled grouse, gobbling and flapping its wings as it took flight, staying low over the heather. Our track dropped out of the cloud and the silence into the heart of the gill. It is a unique trail for many reasons, but the contour-defying rocky singletrack felt out of place in a landscape better known for its wide grassy lanes and gently rolling fellsides.

The descent was over in a flurry of chopping changes in direction. Black crags loomed over a thread of a line set between boulders and loose rocks, so enclosed it was almost a tunnel by the time we reached the base. Immediately in front of us were the ruined remains of buildings that had been built on to man-made platforms of flatter ground. They looked out of place in this seemingly natural place, but the reality is that the entire visible landscape has been shaped by man's touch.

Shouts, singing, chatter, industry. The ghosts of these sounds lie heavily on the landscape, echoing within the valley walls.

The history of lead mining in and around Gunnerside stretches back to at least Roman times. Galena (lead ore) runs in vertical seams across the hillsides, and has been extracted, smelted, and worked to make pipes, roofing, bullets, and hundreds of other things since its discovery. Originally, miners dug simple holes in the ground known as bell pits. Look closely and the acned pockmarks of the earliest mine workings are visible all across the Yorkshire Dales. Then, hushing was used: miners dammed springs up on the moors to create large artificial lakes, then demolished the dams. Torrents of water running down the hillside would strip away all topsoil and loose material, washing it down to the streams in the valley bottom. Hundreds of years later we had picked our way down between these scars, for all the world feeling like we were navigating between natural landslips and features. ▶▶

By the mid-1800s, the Industrial Revolution had expanded the demand for lead. Miners tunnelled deep, following seams far into the hillside, creating mile upon mile of interconnecting tunnels, often linking one dale to the next. As silent as Gunnerside Gill was on this midweek morning, the air would once have been filled by the ceaseless din of picks against rock, echoing out of tunnel openings. There was no mechanisation. Just men, tools, and physical effort. Many of those tools were made by Stephen's ancestors, purchased by the miners, carried to work each day. The smithy also made the carts that would creak under the weight of ore, pulled by boys and horses.

Shouts, singing, chatter, industry. The ghosts of these sounds lie heavily on the landscape, echoing within the valley walls. There's beauty in the delicate skeletal buildings: a slender chimney reaching towards moody skies, empty windows framing the post-industrial relics and the heather-capped fells beyond.

We followed the trail down the valley. Gunnerside Beck widened from a brisk, rock-filled stream to a broader and less hurried course. As we rode, our tyre tracks followed the journey of the lead, and of the miners at the end of the working day – weary, blackened faces returning home. We passed the dressing floor, where the quarried rock was smashed – usually by women and children – and the ore extracted. Finally the ore was smelted down to lead pigs: ingots of metal to be sold on to industries around the world. In order to identify the origin of each pig, the hot metal was struck with a stamp featuring the initials of the mine. It is those very same imprints that mark the smithy door, fresh from the day the stamp was made. The act of hammering it into the wood was visual proof to the purchaser that

the end product was flawless. This small smithy literally left its mark on the Industrial Revolution in the UK and beyond.

The path we rode was, in its own way, a physical reminder of the hundreds of footprints that would have made this journey every day. The village of Gunnerside sits just upstream of the Gunnerside Beck's confluence with the River Swale. The Old Working Smithy is set back from the banks of the beck. Stephen's footwear and a couple of electric light bulbs aside, the smithy is almost identical to the day it opened in 1795: same furnace, same bellows, same anvil, same process. That can't be said of the world outside its characterful front door. The mines were only just profitable in their day, and once cheaper sources of lead were discovered in America and Spain it didn't take long for the hillsides of the Yorkshire Dales to fall silent again, save for the baaing of the hardy Swaledale sheep.

The Calverts' business carried on regardless. Horses still needed shoeing; agricultural tools and machinery needed making and repairing. Eventually demand even for horseshoes died off. In 2021 a working blacksmith feels anachronistic, even in a quiet village like Gunnerside. Stephen, like many of his family before him, splits his time between blacksmithing and running a small farm. Much of his metalworking now is bespoke – ornamental, almost – but still retains functionality. He works the iron blank into a gate latch as we stand there chatting. A fireplace poker set with a stylised ram's head is waiting to be collected by a customer.

'Any true local feels part of the dale,' Stephen says, working deftly. It's part of what keeps him in a trade that he always seemed destined for. He doesn't have many memories of his grandfather; William died when Stephen was young.   ▶▶

One memory is etched in his mind as clearly as the stamps on the smithy door. Five-year-old Stephen was battling with a walnut and a nutcracker, but his small hands were unable to wrap around the handles. William dressed him up in his coat and took him to the smithy. Stephen watched as his grandfather worked the metal, each strike pushing, shaping. It didn't take long before William handed Stephen his own miniature nutcracker. Not many years later, Stephen was helping his father in the smithy. He's still here 40 years on.

Gunnerside's population is significantly lower than it was in its mining heyday. It has declined more rapidly in recent years as people move away to find work and the old cottages are bought up as second homes and holiday lets. There's no bitterness in Stephen's voice as he describes this. He understands that people need work; and who wouldn't want a holiday home in this beautiful part of the world? Instead, he has a sense of pride that he's bucked the trend and maintained a piece of history for another generation. Perhaps, though, he also carries a sense of loss for the close-knit community way of life that has gradually disappeared.

Is Stephen the end of the family line for working blacksmiths in the dale? Well, his teenage daughter has expressed an interest in carrying on the business, so there may still be blacksmith Calverts for another generation. There's an increased relevance to his trade, too. People are once again valuing commodities that last and can be repaired when they do finally break – a step away from the disposable culture of the last few decades.

This trip has been about exploring permanence and transience. The peak of the lead-mining boom lasted just a century, yet its impact on the landscape and the culture of Swaledale will survive much longer. The old mine buildings, the stamps on the smithy door, the hollow worn into its wooden floor, the dents on the anvil, and the trail through Gunnerside are living entities. While they will physically remain for years to come, the stories connected with them need to be retold for them to retain their meaning – and their connection to the stunning landscape in which they are set. History isn't just what is written down in books; it is about people, lives, experiences.

Photography provided courtesy of Orbea

orbea.com // @orbea

@24Tom // @duncanphilpott // @samneedham_photo

Riders: @bexjwills // @jolleyisjolley

The Blessing

Words & Photo: Jess Vincent // Location: Peru

A SINGLE MOMENT

Were it not for her, our windowless mud shelter would soon be in darkness. Killa – an alpaca herder in Peru's Cordillera Vilcanota – wears a parakeet-yellow hat as big as a lampshade. As if in defiance of the setting sun, her jacket shines with bright white buttons and rainbow-coloured alpaca wool, while her hands, cracked and purple like sun-dried leather, move at lightning speed. I'm in awe of how her unprotected fingers effortlessly combine green and yellow threads into a condor in flight, despite sub-zero temperatures and very little light. She, on the other hand, most likely wonders why I can barely grip my cup of coca-leaf tea without trembling, or why I wince as I pull my boots off my blistered feet.

Along with two other climbers, I had been trekking through southern Peru's Cordillera Vilcanota for three days when Kila and her husband found us. Taking pity on our frozen hands and meagre food rations, they'd invited us into their mountain shelter, which they often slept in when herding their alpacas on higher ground. The hut was conveniently located near the foot of Qampa, a 5,500m peak that, all being well with the weather, we were due to summit the next morning.

'You must ask the *apu* [mountain god] for protection,' Killa's husband says after I tell him of our plans to summit Qampa. He's referring to Vilcanota's 6,384m Ausangate peak towering in the distance, a glittering icy jewel and one of the many sacred mountains in Peru believed by the Quechua people to be a living spirit. Without another word, he prepares a small pile of sugar, coca leaves, and scraps of wool, then carefully wraps it in a piece of colourful woven cloth and ushers me to the door.

Outside, the snow-capped mountain god is swallowing the sun whole, turning the icy lakes and mossy rocks around us into liquid sherbet. The cold air hits me like a steel punch to the stomach, but Killa's husband, who I later learn is a respected shaman in the area, seems unaffected as he gets to work assembling a fire. I kneel by the flames and, as the smoke begins to lick my eyes with a stinging burn, the shaman begins chanting in Quechua.

Almost all the words are unintelligible to me, apart from one that's repeated again and again: apu. The shaman places the package he'd prepared on my left shoulder, his eyes closed and his hands trembling as if Ausangate's spirit has entered his body. The cloth bundle swoops past my face and rests on my right shoulder, then on my back and, lastly, on my forehead. He pauses here for a moment, his voice lowering to a whisper barely audible. Eyes open and with a final murmuring of 'apu', the shaman turns and places the offering in the now raging fire, filling the cold twilight air with the smell of burnt wool and caramelised sugar.

'You will be safe,' he says before returning to the hut.

I follow him back into the warmth, where Killa is now removing what looks like an oversized hamster from a pot of boiling water with her bare hands. 'It's *cuy* [guinea pig],' she says while plucking violently at its brown-orange fur. Great chunks of it land on the dirt floor between our feet. She skewers the animal, its mouth agape and eyes frozen in horror, and places it on the fire inside the hut. Cold and ravenous, the five of us stare at the flames in silence.

The meat, charred on the outside but succulent near the bone, is served with purple potatoes that twist and curl at impossible angles. Tomorrow, I will complete my first-ever ice climb – if the mountain gods will it. For now, though, there's nothing left to do but eat to the crackling of burning wood and the audible slicing of air as Killa begins to weave again.

Garibaldi

Words & Photo: Ben Haggar // Location: British Columbia, Canada

Dense clouds roll in, reducing my world to a claustrophobic sphere filled with vertigo. Trying to feel the snow beneath my skis is like reading braille with gloves on. I do my best to adjust to the subtle changes in slope angle, tracking back and forth as I ascend the broad ridge, with Shawn a few metres behind. It soon narrows, and the snow changes from soft supportive powder to firmer wind-scoured ice towards the crest. We're getting close to the summit.

My hood is cinched down against the wind, and the continuous plodding and lack of visual stimulation draw my thoughts inward. It's almost better this way. The surrounding mountains – huge, dispassionate, distant – remind me that, in order to complete our ambitious project, we'll have to climb most of the peaks in sight within the next nine months. It had seemed like a formidable challenge even on paper: 100 summits within the boundaries of Garibaldi Park in the calendar year of 2020. Now the immensity of this task tears at my confidence.

Our reason for climbing 100 peaks is to commemorate the 100th anniversary of this beautiful park in southwestern British Columbia, home to ice fields, alpine ridges, and vast tracts of untouched wilderness. The project seemed like the perfect excuse to explore my home mountain ranges. But, before we had reached our third summit back in January, BC Parks dug a little further into their archives and deduced that – due to a technicality – they would officially be celebrating the centenary in 2027. Our idea was shot.

Undeterred, Shawn and I kept at it as if nothing had changed, but the mountains thought otherwise. Avalanche conditions danced between considerable and high with short forays into extreme – not advisable for winter ski mountaineering. Storms and poor visibility slowed our progress to little more than a crawl. From our first twelve summits, we could only see from two of them.

The wind increases and the angle steepens as the ridge narrows, terminating in a sharp point – the summit. The whys and hows of our project swirl in my head like the snow billowing off the ridge and stinging my exposed face. Sastrugi sculpted into beautiful patterns provide the only grip as we switch from skinning to bootpacking and take turns standing on the sharp snow-crusted pinnacle of Diamond Head. Gravity provides the only point of reference as the steep snow slopes merge with the fog. Sky, ground, and horizon combine as one indistinguishable tone of light grey as I wobble unsteadily for my obligatory summit photo.

For those brief minutes my thoughts are free from burden. Little exists here except for the wind and the cold and the tiny speck of accomplishment at reaching summit 13 of 100. Slowly chipping away at our momentous task is all we can do. We are wildly behind our schedule of 1.92 peaks per week, but we bank on our ability to make up ground in the longer days of better weather and stable snow offered by the spring months ahead. We have no way of knowing that, with an imminent lockdown and park closure lasting six months, this will be our second-to-last summit for a long while. Would knowledge of this have changed my light-hearted elation? Possibly, but what really matters in this moment are the smiles shared between friends, the bond acquired from shared physical hardships, and feeling the raw power of the elements in this hostile winter storm.

@benhaggarphoto

SURVIVAL L

N PARADISE

STORY & PHOTOGRAPHY: TERENCE VER ANGSIOCO
WRITTEN BY: MEGAN BROWNRIGG
LOCATION: CORON ISLAND

'We forgot the serving spoon.'

Wielding a machete isn't the response I expect from Chef Hilven, but he's a solutions kind of guy. To the crackled blare of Bob Marley's *Give Me Love*, he aggressively starts hacking away at a tube of bamboo. Splinters slice into the sand like drunk arrows, but Hilven's cavalier cool suggests this is how he always sources his cutlery. He's well aware that his heroism is being caught on camera, but I'm happy to film and swoon. My new bro makes something out of nothing daily. He cuts problems down to size. Finds wealth in weird places. Today's win is the abandoned cove he's brought us to – the set for our latest episode of *Island Cooking*. The sand strip is guarded by sheer limestone cliffs that lean over us like policemen. Clutches of forest sprout from the rock, suspended in mid-air, peering with green jealousy at the ocean below. These open waters braid inlets through Coron Island's cliffs, widening into lagoons inland – teal lakes considered sacred by the Tagbanua people. They're also wrapped in tribal stories, and their exact locations are kept secret from outsiders. It's a hell of a back yard for Hilven.

The chef crouches over our clay pot like a kidney bean. I turn our blackened fish across the burning twigs, which click as they grill. Naked flames mash with midday sun to bake us both in the haze. But our Instagram Live is rolling and we act cool as cucumbers, playing Bob Marley on LOOP. 'HELLO and welcome to another episode of island cooking with your hosts Terencito and Chef Hilven!' I sing into my iPhone. 'Today's special is Sigang – fish with onion, mango, ginger, and tamarind leaves: no additives!' Hilven cuts

a cashew nut for its sour flesh and I spin round to give a panorama of our location. Behind us, Coron Island's waters sit glassy still, as if they could never be splintered by wind.

This sea tells lies. During the typhoon that first let me explore this place, I've watched the Sulu Sea build walls before smashing into liquid shards. As a boy, I'd sail past the Filipino island on family holidays, thinking that its towering mountains looked like the back of a dragon. I'd see its tiny huts sitting on thin lines of white sand and wonder who lived in them. But everyone knows that Coron Island, and its surrounding ocean, belong to the Tagbanua tribe. You need the permission of tribal elders to step foot on its shores. I'd turn 39 before earning that privilege.

Thanks to a social enterprise that partners with the Tagbanuas, I was lucky enough to visit Coron Island in November 2019. There was no big moment of meeting the tribe. They're modern people. But, when a storm stopped anyone else from accessing the island, I got some alone time with them. As a city boy from Makati, I assumed that we were all going to run out of supplies and die in the typhoon. I gallantly shared my eggs, instant noodles, and rum with the Tagbanuas, having no concept that these guys can catch their own food whenever they want. Still, the popular taste of MSG got me an invite to the bar. I spent an evening watching the tribe's courtship dance of *suring*. The man's goal is to face the woman, who will nimbly twist her hands above her head, like a gentle jazz hand, whilst shuffling her feet and keeping her face turned away from him. My time to shine came when I was invited to win one elderly woman's heart. It was a brief affair;

▶▶

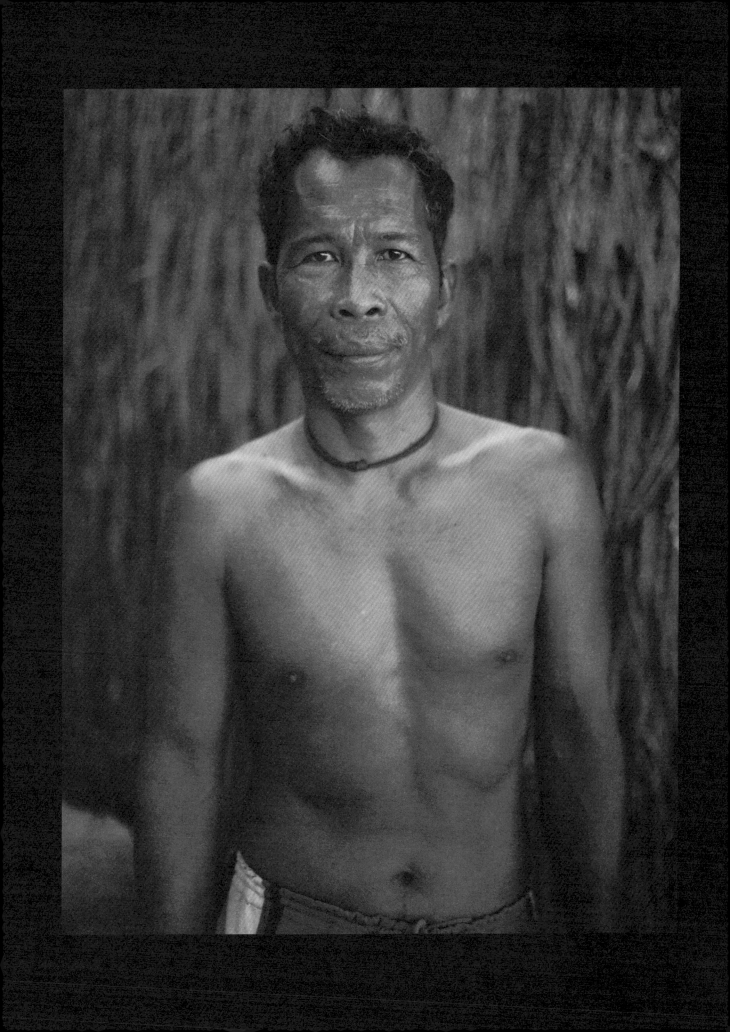

my quickest boxing moves proved nothing to her slow but perfectly timed pirouettes. Learning that she was happily married afterwards iced my bruised ego.

***

Later that evening, I battled collective boredom with my Bluetooth speaker. Taking a risk on my street cred, I played criminally cheesy Filipino songs to my new friends. There's something about our country's pop music that is full of real feeling but also unapologetically uncool. Maybe it's the ardour of a poorer nation putting our problems into songs. What I did not know is that the Tagbanua tribe would go completely mad for the karaoke classics. *Loved* them. Singing and dancing together in the storm, we belted out notes of hope and heartache together, and I felt at home.

In all the silly that night, a serious moment did come. A village elder, called an *Apo* (grandad), suddenly got emotional. He started telling me his dream for his grandson, Gilbert, to finish school. I learned that someone finishing school in the tribe is very, very rare and even if it happens, things will be difficult. The Tagbanuas welcomed me and my terrible playlists with open arms but they rarely receive the same hospitality, even from their neighbouring islands. The tribe walk barefoot, they're darker, and they get looks when they cross to town. This Apo knew that his grandson might never finish school. Drunk and passionate, I wanted to promise I could fix this, that I could help Gilbert. But such promises aren't a good idea, and these things aren't about money. Instead, we kept dancing together. I kept taking photos.

When the weather calmed a few days later, I left the Tagbanuas. Chef Hilven is in my pictures from that night in the bar, but I didn't know his name back then. Despite being touched by the tribe, these people were still strangers in my memory. This stayed the case for months, until I packed a bag and asked permission to go back to Coron Island. I wanted to know more about the people I'd danced with in that storm. This tribe who owned an ocean.

***

My second visit to the island lasted 66 days. During this time, I learned that the Tagbanuas are masters of their universe. Living in an ancestral domain, free of government jurisdiction, they're everything in one: spearfishers, farmers, foragers, even their own mechanics. The men fish together, sharing one boat and the cost of gasoline. The women harvest the wild yams together in the mountains. No-one overfishes or overharvests, and there's an unwritten rule that if someone has too much of something, they'll share it. When they aren't working, the Tagbanuas kick back together. On long afternoons, the tribe will watch old movies on their shared VCD player. Sometimes they've watched that same movie 15 times already, but it never loses its magic. The tribe also fight like family. When one elder gets bored of smoked fish, he swaggers into the ocean with his spear, sulkily stabbing his own fresh catch.

Initially blindsided by the idea of 'paradise', it took me time to learn that the tribe's civil freedom didn't come easy to them. These people who own an ocean are warriors of their island's well-being – warriors who fought fiercely for their rights. Back in the '80s, Coron was exploited by investors for the swifts' nests in its caves and for the fish in its waters. The sacred lakes were poisoned with cyanide, and families were evicted from the coves they'd lived in for generations. The Tagbanuas were at serious risk of losing their home until they were finally awarded their Certificate of Ancestral Domain Claim (CADC) under the Indigenous People's Rights Act in 2001. With its intimate network of

▶ ▶

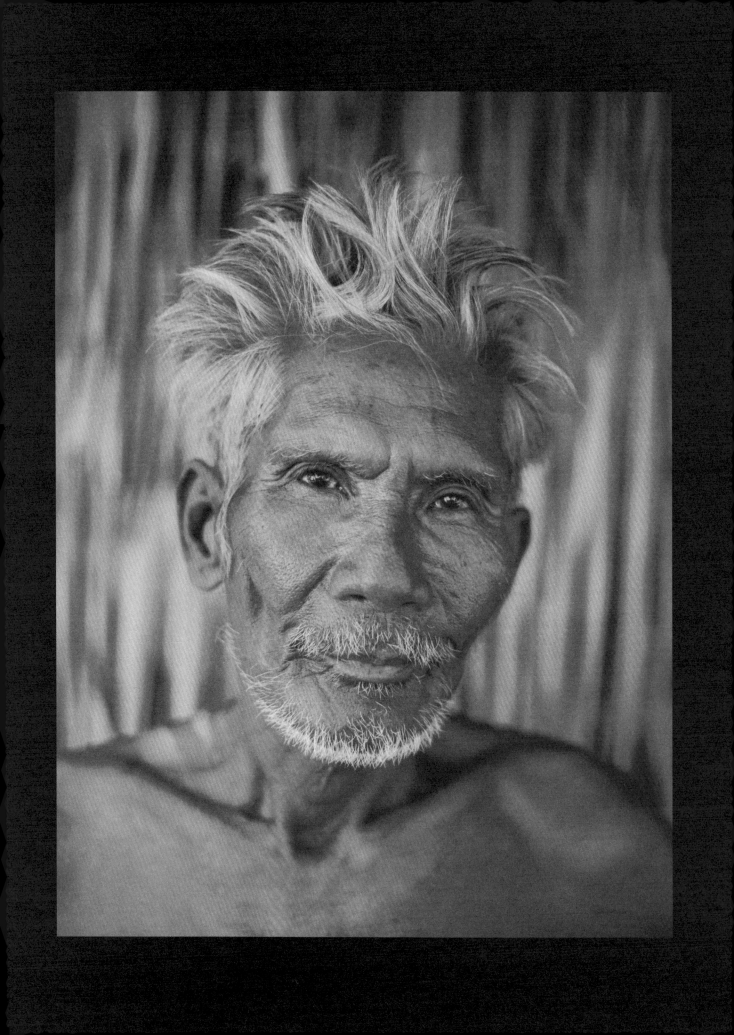

lagoons, Coron became the first territory in the world where rights over the ocean were recognised. Today, the Tagbanuas don't need anyone to survive apart from each other.

On my second visit, noticing the tribe's self-sufficiency, I felt silly for arriving with half a supermarket, including tinned tuna. To hoover up the evidence, I started using up ingredients by presenting a fake cookery show with my iPhone. Although I speak the same language as the Tagbanuas, I recorded the episodes in English for my family and friends. My corny lines and Bob Marley soundtrack attracted the curiosity of Chef Hilven, who also speaks the language. Hilven was so shy at first that I didn't expect a bromance to blossom. His strong bushy eyebrows and slight moustache reveal his maturity at 21, but they don't hide his inquisitive baby face, or his habit of quickly looking away when he's unsure. His eyes are full of sea salt; their roasted nut brown conveys his warmth. But they're steely too, as if they've never quite rinsed out the ocean. With his powerful ability to cross cultures, Hilven asked to be my co-host. I was buzzing.

I soon learned that Hilven's shyness has limits. On his afternoons off, he was perfectly happy to showcase his flawless abs by posing for photos in the sea's shallows. He would wag his head with a boyish smile if he knew that a punchline was in reach. But Hilven is also an amazing formally trained chef. Together we made everything from vegan bowls to fish curry and pumpkin coconut pancakes (which we both admitted were terrible). When we weren't filming or cooking, we'd sing karaoke or talk. Trouble is, Hilven's big-hearted ease was so easy to be around that he'd lulled me into thinking he was a guy without problems. But our chats dug up that Hilven had never got to finish school. He talked a lot about wishing he had. He's such a strong spearfisher that his cove needs him in the ocean. One afternoon, perched on a paddleboard, I got to witness why.

Chef Hilven's freediving is proof that the Tagbanuas are superhuman. That guy was like a flying ballerina underwater. Spear in hand, Hilven's goofiness evaporated as his lithe body hit depths of more than 30ft in one breath. In the open ocean, he reached a new meditative state, mentally and spiritually exploring an uncharted world. Without jarring its serenity, he pointed his spear at a fish and pierced it with one body shot. I didn't expect him to bite into the fish's brain afterwards. Its tail spasmed as a cloud of red blood released into the water. A deadly love story with tantalising visuals, spearfishing is the greatest survival show on Earth. Watching Hilven in the ocean was like seeing Michael Jordan play basketball and thinking *I want to play like Mike*.

As the Tagbanua intern, I was up for trying to hunt my own food, even if it involved propelling myself underwater with a gun I didn't know how to use. Hilven approached the role of teacher by pointing to a rock at the ocean's bottom and saying 'Go there, sir!' Although I'd practised a bit of freediving closer to shore, this tuition from Hilven felt quite hands off. His shouts of 'Sir, just relax! Relax!' also didn't help. But I did my breathing exercises, harnessed a scrap of calm, and dived. I gently kicked my body down, down and down, feeling elated at what I was doing. Down, down, down, then, *NO, fuck fuck fuck I can't do it!* Paralysed by fear halfway, I swallowed a mouthful of seawater and choked my way back to the surface. Hilven was in creases. 'What are you doing, sir?' he cried in hysterics. 'You need to relax!' ▶ ▶

'That's impossible!' I spluttered in anger. 'You're pushing me too hard!' Hilven held his stomach in glee. Taking confidence from his complete lack of concern, I told myself that I wouldn't die and I didn't need air. I headed back down, this time keeping a steady direction with minimal thinking. Down, down, down. Down. Down. *Oh my god! It's working!* Suddenly, I was in my own *Zero to Hero* movie and my life arc was peaking OUT. Spotting a sleepy fish in my euphoria, I carefully cocked the speargun so it didn't backfire into my crotch – one thing Hilven had warned me about. My head screamed in silent excitement when I hit it. I pushed to the water's surface with my tiny fish, yelping 'I CAN FEED MYSELF!' Hilven found my euphoria just as hilarious as my near drowning. The underwater world is a baptism of fire.

***

Our spearfishing harvest is what brings us to the abandoned cove, to cook our catches. But after filming our Insta-Live, the glint in Hilven fades for a moment. He tells me he's going off fish and just wants to eat spaghetti. Although I've seen him rule the ocean today, I'm reminded that Hilven is at home, not in paradise. Watching him freedive through cathedrals of sunlit water might staggeringly spiritual, but it's also an act of survival. Just like me, Hilven longs for access to new worlds. He wants to meet his favourite actor in Manila, to cook in urban hotels, to go to school. Knowing I can't promise him any of this, I distract Hilven with comments from today's *Island Cooking* episode. I groan as endless exclamations of how much everyone loves Chef Hilven fill my screen. He knocks me out with another single sentence: 'I can't believe foreigners care about me.' The sun dips to a gluey amber as he pours salt from a shell over our meal. 'Wow. It feels so good to be appreciated!' My mind floats uncomfortably in what he's said, but Hilven breaks into a proud toothy smile, proffering his handmade bamboo spoon to serve our food. This young Tagbanua lives off the gifts of his island. Problems pass across his mind, like shifting clouds, and he goes on living.

@terencever // @brownriggmegan

Sand in the Blood

WORDS & PHOTOGRAPHY: SIMON URWIN
LOCATION: ALGERIA

The immigration official asks if I'm a journalist or a spy. I tell him I'm neither. After a stern grilling, he stamps my entry papers – which have taken four tortuous months to organise – before directing me on to his colleagues in customs. There, two men in uniform pick through my luggage.

'You have a drone or binoculars? We always confiscate them if we find them,' one of them warns. I shake my head. 'Why are you here, anyway?' asks the other. 'I've always wanted to visit Tassili n'Ajjer,' I reply. 'I'm told it's the most beautiful desert in the world.'

Eventually they wave me through. From the capital Algiers I head south under police escort – a requirement for all foreigners travelling by road in Algeria, partly due to the country's fondness for red tape, but mostly because of the suspicion that surrounds any visit to the frontier zone with Libya and Niger, where the vast volcanic plateau of Tassili n'Ajjer lies.

Some 1,800km later, in the town of Illizi, I'm handed over to a team of Tuaregs, the nomadic people of the Sahara. Hassan the driver, Moulay the cook, and Tito the guide await me in their four-by-four, all of them sporting the traditional *tagelmust*: the veil-turban that serves as both desert protection and symbol of Tuareg identity. We load the vehicle with supplies for the coming weeks before setting out on tarmac buckled by the searing heat of summer. Road signs warn of deadly curves and dangerous conditions ahead, but we pick up speed regardless. 'The desert must be respected, but if you love it, it will be kind to you. So never fear it,' Tito says as we veer off road onto a dry lakebed, the sound of our engine sending a herd of wild camels running for cover behind a thicket of Saharan myrtles.

The mobile phone signal soon disappears. We carry no maps, nor satnav; Tito navigates on instinct alone. 'We Tuaregs are born with an ability to read the desert like a sixth sense,' he tells me. 'We believe that this information is passed down genetically from our nomadic forefathers. Our parents and grandparents teach us too. By night I use the stars, and by day I find my way using landmarks and by following old watercourses. I never use the sand dunes, though. They are restless and always on the move, just like the Tuareg.'

We pull up for the night in the lee of a dune that stands 700m high. Tents are pitched, a fire is lit, and the important ritual of tea making gets underway. 'Just as the French have their wine, so we have our green tea,' Tito says while filling a pot with leaves, sugar, and water, then placing it amongst the flames. 'It is known as the friend of conversation, and an invitation to take tea is considered a sign of respect,' he adds before boiling and aerating the liquid three times. He pours me a cup. 'Key to good tea is a sugary, foamy top. Tea without froth is like a Tuareg without his turban.'

We wake at sunrise and set out along an *oued*, a dry riverbed, and edge our way into Tassili n'Ajjer – a startling, otherworldly region of rock and sand that covers an area twice the size of Belgium. At every turn we encounter great cathedrals of sandstone violently sculpted, shattered, and splintered by the elements. Natural arches soar

▶▶

skyward all around us; there are more than 300 in this area alone. Every viewpoint is more astonishing than the last. On one afternoon we crest a ridge to find the most beautiful of them all: a lunar plain known as the Mountains That Echo, where mesas and buttes are marooned in multicoloured waves of sand on all points of the compass, like multiple Monument Valleys.

For days, we are utterly alone. There are only the faintest traces of other life: the tracks of a jackal outside our tents one morning; the discarded skins of a knot of vipers now hibernating beneath the sand. Yet, incredibly, this stark landscape once teemed with life. 'Some time ago, the Sahara was green savannah, abundant in wildlife,' Tito says as we scramble to the back of a cave to see a pictograph of an antelope hunt painted in a mixture of blood, milk, and powdered rock.

'We know from the rock art that at least ten thousand years ago there were many different animals here, including elephants, crocodiles, lions, and rhinoceroses,' he says. 'Four thousand years later, the desert dwellers documented the cattle they farmed and the giraffes they kept for their milk. And as the land became drier, around three thousand years ago, they made carvings of the camels that passed through on the trans-Saharan caravans. So the art is like a history book. It shows us how the climate changed and how humankind adapted.'

The days pass and we venture slowly south, with stops to dig ourselves out of the sand, fix a tyre, or to collect water from *gueltas*, the desert's hidden pockets of water. We spend our nights around the fire, sharing stories over bowls of couscous prepared by Moulay in his makeshift desert kitchen. 'Tonight we are in a haunted place,' Tito says after we set camp near a spot called the Cave of Imorouden. 'A Tuareg woman who died in childbirth is buried nearby. The cries of her baby can sometimes be heard at night, so don't be surprised if your sleep is disturbed. Occasionally people wake and find the prints of a crawling infant in the sand. The desert may appear lifeless, but it is full of spirits.'

As we head deeper into the wilderness, the sand passes through a mind-bending spectrum of colours – from bone white to gold, then deep orange and blood red. The rock art becomes more detailed too. There are water maps written in the ancient Tuareg language, Tamasheq; images of people dancing; even what appears to be a set of prehistoric games, similar to checkers, carved in a table of rock. 'This area was once so rich in prey and food that it gave the people free time to think and draw,' Tito says while scattering sand over a block of pink granite, then blowing away the surplus to reveal the image of a horned steer hidden in its surface. 'We see not only early forms of creative expression but also self-reflection – of, perhaps for the very first time, humans understanding their place in the world. Today, it is still a place to do much the same thing. The desert is a place to stop and think.'

We eventually reach journey's end in Tassili n'Ajjer's southernmost tip, close to the Algerian border with Libya. Here the threat from ISIS is referred to euphemistically as 'stormy weather', but it's taken very seriously, and we turn back. We head for the oasis settlement of Djanet, 200km away, where I am due to catch the long flight home, and Tito will spend some time with his family. 'It will be only a few short weeks before I am back in Tassili,' he tells me en route. 'I am a Tuareg, after all. The sand is in my blood and in my bones. Here is where I feel a true sense of home and belonging. I am drawn to it like the pull of a magnet. Many people who visit Tassili n'Ajjer also come to feel the same.'

@simonurwinphoto

Polar Shadows

Winter in the Svalbard Archipelago

WORDS & PHOTOGRAPHY: VINCENT COLLIARD // CAROLINE CÔTÉ
LOCATION: SPITSBERGEN

I first met Caroline, a Canadian adventure filmmaker, in Antarctica. One evening, sitting on a sled in front of the Gerlache Strait bordering the Antarctic Peninsula, we lit a cigarillo – and the flame started burning. Two years later we committed ourselves to an attempt at the first unsupported, full-length winter traverse of Spitsbergen, the main island of the Svalbard archipelago. We knew that the Polar Shadows expedition would be hard. This is a tale of suffering and exhaustion in the darkness and screaming winds – a tale of an uncertain future.

Njørd, the god of the wind, forces us to submit in the end. Now we have no alternative but to pitch our tent on the edge between the sea ice and the glacier. Everything, absolutely everything, is totally white. And wild. I have a gnawing feeling about that low pressure coming from the open ocean – it's bound to change our lives, and not for the better.

I have always known that the appreciation of a journey is greater when we have no idea about the outcome. For me, the absolute commitment of going unsupported represents the purest essence of adventure and exploration. But I have to remind myself of this again and again as the ferocious wind tears at our tent and we huddle there in the dark, trying desperately to conserve body heat.

***

Seven weeks earlier

Dawn – or something like it. It's midday at the beginning of February, and a dim glow lights up the distant horizon. The twilight immediately overlaps the dawn here at 78 degrees north. We only have three hours of poor visibility left after collecting the last pieces of equipment from the post office, so we begin pulling our sleds along the Advent Valley, loaded up with nearly 300kg of food, fuel, and equipment shared between the two of us. Our progress feels extremely slow, but I have to remind myself that our priority at this early stage is not mileage but to listen to our bodies. We have a long way to travel.

***

Our skis glide across ice-carved valleys, the mystical fjords, and the frozen plateaus. After one month in the field, our routine has become a near-perfect machine. Caroline and I accomplish our daily tasks like two programmed robots. Partly this is a response to the fact that we can't hear each other most of the time – the wind, ceaselessly bombarding the multiple layers covering our heads, has plunged us each into a bubble of isolation. Evenings in the tent are dominated by the roar of the stove, and our energy is too low to overcome it. So we save ourselves from conversation.

Instead we trust the technique used by the polar bears, setting aside every calorie for a precise purpose. When they hunt, a task requiring an immense commitment of energy, they need to be sure of success in order to reach their prey. In such a vast territory there is no room for error. I look at Caroline, bundled up in down clothing and hunched over a steaming pot, stabbing at the food hungrily with her spoon. She scrapes every last morsel from the pot and licks the spoon afterwards, then shares a look with me – half a smile. I know her. For Caroline, the all-encompassing magnitude of the adventure itself, of meeting the objective, means carrying as little weight as possible. With her past as an ultra-trail runner, she knows the importance of moving lightly without anything superfluous.

'Maybe I made a mistake,' she says aloud, shocking me out of my meditative slump, 'in refusing to carry just a few more kilograms of soup, oatmeal, cereal bars.'

Later, I feel her awake at night. Her body is shaking. Each day we are burning more calories than we consume, and she can't sleep. The demands of moving in the thick snow, fighting to make forward progress, stopping ourselves from

▶▶

sinking into the powder, are building up a calorific deficit that grows day by day.

**

The spectacular green polar lights swirl and vibrate to the sound of no music. Aurora dances against a navy backdrop over this vast landscape of peaks and crevasses, snowfields and silence, painting colours of extraordinary beauty and subtlety over the snows. This territory is known as the Atomfjella Glacier, where many of the mountains have names inspired by nuclear physics: Elektronfjellet, Radiumfjellet. These are the last evenings of the polar night. Soon the sun will return, banishing the aurora, but tonight the magical lights fascinate me, and I gaze into eternity for endless minutes. It is the first time since the beginning of this journey that I have taken a moment to just stand and look at the beauty around us.

We reach the plateau with the spectacular name of Åsgard, which in the old Norwegian language implies that it is the home of the Nordic gods. We wonder if these mythic figures will let us travel across the ice cap. Their power here is palpable, but I can't think about anything other than details, details, more details. Progress, degrees, minutes, seconds. There is no room for compromise – or for romance. We are on a mission. *Am I carrying the short climbing skins on my body to keep the glue at the right temperature? Do I have a fuel pump on me, warm and ready, in case the stove doesn't start? Is the rifle to hand in the sled and easy to pull out?* So goes the list of questions in my head. We don't speak. Caroline skis beside me but I cannot see her face beneath her hood.

**

I wake once again aware that Caroline is shivering uncontrollably. The thermometer reads -38 degrees C inside the tent. New questions flush through my mind. Will we be able to control our fingers and toes in such deep cold? How much harder will it make everything that was already so hard before?

'We should wait for a bit this morning,' I say, and I can hardly understand my own words as they slur out through my lips. 'Maybe it'll get a bit warmer.'

Caroline sits upright in her sleeping bag and looks at me. 'How are your feet?'

They have been suffering. The cold is brutal. Sometimes there is pain, but sometimes there is nothing at all.

Even the effort of skiing cannot warm me up today, and I accelerate my pace to try and generate more body heat, but that is a dangerous tactic in the Arctic winter. The sweat on my body transforms into ice. Now I am even more at risk from hypothermia. The wind howling over the ice cap seems to cut through every single layer to chill my body to the core. I try not to think about my feet. Caroline turns to me after a while and says something, but I can't hear her over the wind.

'We should get down off the ice cap,' I shout to her. 'My feet can't take it. It will be warmer at lower elevations and maybe we can go faster on the fjord ice.'

Now we go straight north along a fjord located 1,000m below. Pitching the tent feels like a struggle, and it is not a safe place; we have to keep our ears open for the heavy footsteps of bears. It is another layer of overhead added to the mental and physical burden we already share. Despite the need to remain vigilant, we both drop off to sleep almost immediately after devouring our evening meals, which fill us and warm our always-hungry bellies.

Our wish for warmer conditions is granted in the cruellest way when, approaching the southern tip of the archipelago, icy rain arrives along with temperatures climbing towards freezing. We are simply not prepared for dealing with moisture. Down must be kept dry, as must electronics, and the only option is to stuff our

▶▶

precious equipment inside our vapour barriers, which we sleep in every night. These impermeable membranes prevent water vapour from condensing in down sleeping bags and turning into big blocks of ice – an essential strategy in the Arctic winter.

***

Despite the challenges, our progress is good until we reach the infamous bay of Isbukta where the weather becomes calm – surprisingly calm. 'I can't quite believe how the conditions have changed,' I tell Caroline, and she nods her amazed agreement. But a communication comes in from Lars Ebbessen, our meteorologist back in Norway: 'You have to hurry before it gets too bad again. There are only a few hours of stability – be careful.'

Instinctively I feel that we are on the verge of experiencing the worst conditions of the expedition so far. As Caro accelerates over the ice I see that she feels the same. We don't have much time. And, after a calm interval so brief that it shocks us both, the wind once more begins to pick up, the snow blasts in with it, and temperatures spiral back down towards deeper cold.

We are moving on a large patch of ice fragmented with scattered holes and icy mounds – tricky to navigate even in clear conditions, but now, with blowing snow increasingly taking over the landscape, I have to fight to orient myself. Snowflakes cake my glasses. My vision is playing tricks on me. Caroline, a yeti-like figure in front, shows no sign of hesitation, and I sense that she is determined to continue. After all, we have no choice but to move forward – to take one more step, and then another, and another. There is no perfect place to set up camp in this hostile environment. We just have to take shelter no matter where we are. My fear is that we will not be able to pitch our tent.

Caro takes the shovel out of the sled. Every gesture is complex now, with the wind roaring against us at 30m/s, plastering us with snow and pushing us back, turning the shovel into a sail. Every stroke shovelling consumes precious energy. The wind is so strong that we can barely stand up. I am beyond exhausted, and in Caro's increasingly sluggish movements I see that she is also drawing from dwindling reserves of strength. Like two zombies, we finally drag ourselves inside the tent and feel temporarily safe for a little while. Wind batters the fabric above our heads and we take the opportunity to swallow a few protein bars before falling stiffly into our sleeping bags.

The stove's flame flickers, and I hope that its comforting glow appeases my partner's gloomy thoughts in these weather conditions. Although she hasn't said so, she must be sharing my doubts about the outcome of this great challenge. But we are a solid team. I know that she can do it. This is not the only time we have been mentally and physically tested during the Polar Shadows expedition; on countless occasions we have had to trust each other and move forward. Tonight, when the winds are shrieking around us, I need her to continue to believe and to keep a positive spirit burning. More than ever, we must be united. I want to say all of these things to her and more, but we both lie there in silence – conserving, always conserving. Perhaps she is thinking the same thoughts about me.

At midnight I realise that I hear nothing in the tent. No howling wind, no drumbeat of snow on the fabric. How is it possible? Lars had told us about strong winds raging through the night. I hear Caro's voice breaking through my thoughts: 'Vincent, we're getting buried.' ▶ ▶

“

Vincent, we're getting buried.

She reaches out of her sleeping bag and pushes against the thin tent walls. Nothing. There is a solidity, now, to the atmosphere, and I feel a pulse of claustrophobia like a cold hand pressing against my chest. *The walls are covered with an immense amount of snow.* With growing trepidation I realise that we will need to be efficient in order to get out of here.

We put our whole bodies to work, arms and feet scrambling to dig through the absurd quantity of packed snow blocking the entrance and flattening the roof. *Will the tent poles be able to endure all this weight? What happens if they can't?* I manage to make my way to the surface, 2m higher, but I have to jump to get my whole body out, squirming and swimming through the snow. I can't believe it. Outside our pit, the storm is still driving long streamers of snow over this landscape of pure white. With wet snow piling up against us we take turns to clear it as it covers the tent again and again. Ice plates grow like lesions over our bodies. Our clothes become blocks of ice.

I make eye contact with Caro. Her eyes are the only part of her I can see through the snow that seems to have colonised her entire body. Together, we give everything – we keep moving forward, keep striving, keep going a little further.

In the morning, after calm returns, I take my indelible pencil and write on the inner wall of the tent: *somehow we made it.*

After 63 days and 1,123km, Vincent and Caroline successfully completed the first unsupported double winter crossing of the main island of Spitsbergen: Longyearbyen to the northern tip of the island, from the northern tip the southern tip, then back to Longyearbyen. They reached Sorkapp at the southernmost point on March 20, one day before the end of winter. @vincentcolliard // @caro.line.cote

POINTS

OF *CONTACT*

Our world is stone
Shaped by water and wind and time
It sweats when it's hot
And sticks when it's cold
It's the place where we gather
And tape our fingers
And huddle together to wait out storms
Where we've learned to try hard
And learned to fail
And sometimes succeed
Learned when to hold on
And when to let go

We've made families here
Shared beta
Returned each season, year after year
Finding our wildness in wild places
Spoken its language
Studied its cracks and fissures
Its imperfections and its characters
The moves that make up each route
The climbs that make up a life
The voices that make up a community
The ones that call us back
Home

patagonia®

Aletsch Glacier, Switzerland Tourism / Frederic Huber

I need a change of scenery.

Switzerland.

Discover Switzerland now: **MySwitzerland.com**

Tell us about your favourite experiences using **#IneedSwitzerland**

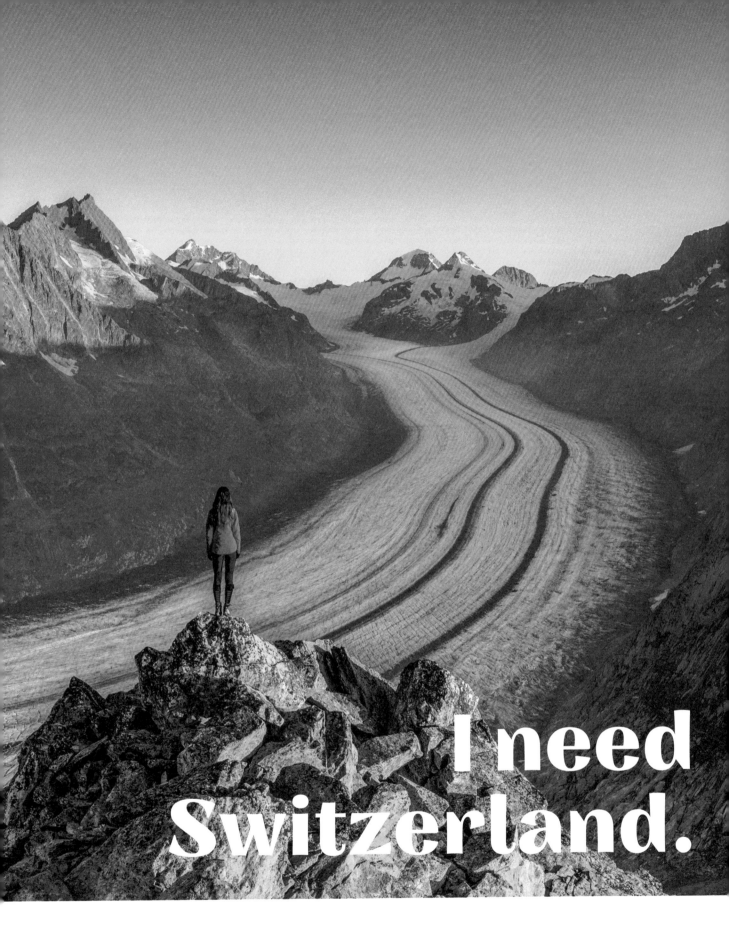

I need
Switzerland.